The Sociology of Planning

Lynnette Carey
Research Associate
University of Keele

Roy Mapes
Director
Statistical Research Unit in Sociology
University of Keele

The Sociology of Planning

A Study of Social Activity on New Housing Estates

B. T. Batsford Ltd   London

First published 1972
© Lynnette Carey and Roy Mapes 1972

Made and printed in Great Britain by
C. Tinling & Co. Ltd, London and Prescot
for the publishers B. T. Batsford Ltd
4 Fitzhardinge Street, London W.1

ISBN 0 7134 0961 4

Contents

Preface

Architects and planners often refer to the need to 'design for living'. This is a rather hackneyed phrase which like most institutionalised expressions falls all too easily from the tongue. However, if an architect is really concerned with the way in which a realised design is used and enjoyed by the people who will have to experience it as a part of their lives, then the architect must become something of a sociologist or must at least employ one. The planner may claim that a person's ecological surroundings are the most powerful factors influencing his happiness. The economist may claim that the ease with which he may pay for what he has will make or mar his enjoyment of life. The sociologist will rightly point out that he has a need for the company of others and the extent to which this is satisfied will also figure strongly in his happiness.

This book is very much concerned with the process by which social relationships were established on a number of new owner-occupier estates. If one thinks about it, the whole business of settling in to a new house can be an important and not necessarily a pleasant experience. Apart from countless operational frustrations and the fact that the choice may have been a compromise anyway, there is the important fact that a great number of new householders are complete strangers to the area in which the new home is situated. As a consequence neither husband nor wife have friends or acquaintances at the point of moving in. The husband may more easily develop friendships quickly because of his work situation. The wife is often effectively tied to a new estate and obviously can remain friendless. In this book we are interested in tracing the way in which the 'new' housewife builds up her relationships with others on the estate.

There is a criticism of the way we have handled our empirical work which we will anticipate. Although we have certainly paid attention to housewives' friendships off the estate and their maintained links with friends and relatives we have largely ignored such things in our analysis. For this reason it might be claimed that our treatment is too clinical, even artificial. Our defence against this is that while we were interested in the process whereby friendships develop over time, we were also interested in the specific influence of the estate character itself on this process. For example, one of our interests was how the dispositions of the houses themselves influenced the setting up of friendship links. We argue that under such conditions we needed to focus somewhat and exclude the wider scene, however interesting. While we utter a note of apology for the somewhat clinical nature of our research design, we do not apologise at all for making full use of the advantages which such a design offers.

Any research in the social sciences, it is said may be defined as on a continuum from loose but 'important' to tight but 'trivial'; or so it is popularly held. We challenge the truth of this to some extent. Although wide-reaching, large, loosely constructed pieces of work often yield valuable insights, they are, despite their size, too uncontrolled to permit generalisation to the population with any confidence. The traditional attitude to research at the other end of the continuum is that so much has to be controlled that any such study becomes sterile. People are reduced to numbers and the full, rich flavour of social reality is lost.

In this research we have tended to the 'tight' end of the continuum. We have done this, first, because it is our natural inclination so to do. But, second, because we have been surprised by the lack of consistency in many of the past research studies in this field.

Actually, it is no longer necessary to be trivial just because one's control is tight. The growth of statistical methods has made it possible to apply control of the factors which interfere with that which one wishes to isolate, *after* the research is completed.

Preface

This means that one observes and records as much as possible and then holds constant all the interfering variables, focussing only on the one which is at present of interest.

In order to achieve such control yet not to interfere with the entirely normal social processes on the estates, we have used control after the research. Inevitably we wish that we had recorded more, e.g. our use of social psychological measures is inadequate and we regret the omissions. Nevertheless, by and large, we have succeeded in drawing a number of conclusions which may be useful to planners and which have a fair degree of validity. Such confidence in the validity of our results can only be bought at a price. The price in this research has been the necessary use of some quite difficult statistical methods. There should be some qualification at this stage: to a statistician the methods we have used are customary, not at all difficult and are the ones he would expect to see used. However, empirical sociological analysis has lagged woefully behind some of the other social sciences in the techniques used and strategies adopted. This, it is stressed, has implications for the validity of a number of past urban sociological researches on grounds of analysis alone – let alone that weakness in initial definition and operationalisation touched upon previously.

We do not then apologise for making use of such techniques; we feel that most empirical sociology will be using such statistical methods fairly soon. On the other hand we are sensitive to the difficulties that many people have in these areas. Accordingly, we have included an extensive glossary on the meanings of the statistical principles drawn upon and although most of the book can be read through skipping the statistics, we feel that assiduous use of the glossary will help the reader to a fuller and more satisfying understanding.

In order to carry out the research which led to the writing of this book, the assistance of certain agencies and individuals was essential. We gratefully acknowledge the help of the various offices of the Staffordshire, Cheshire and Stoke-on-Trent Planning Authorities. In particular, the help of Miss Mary Burns, Stafford and Mr J. W. Plant, Stoke-on-Trent.

The financial assistance of first of all the University of Keele and later the Social Science Research Council is gratefully acknowledged.

Finally the reader will realize that our research design was something of a gamble in that it was essential to secure as near a 100 per cent response from our householders as possible. Our grateful thanks are due to these North Staffordshire householders who helped our gamble to pay off.

1 Introduction

The elementary family in contemporary industrial society

The elementary or nuclear family may be defined as the small group consisting of the husband, his wife and their dependent children. The manner in which this type of family is adapting to the demands of contemporary industrial society is being currently discussed by sociologists and social anthropologists alike. Much of the debate so far has centred on the relationship between the elementary and extended families. Attempts have been made to demonstrate that the 'traditional' functions of the extended family have been modified because of the necessity for individual mobility. However, the extent to which this changed role has affected the behaviour of the elementary family at its territorial base – the neighbourhood – has not been widely examined systematically. This is particularly true in the U.K. The concern of this book is the behaviour of the elementary family, and more especially of the housewife, in this residential setting.

If the elementary family is indeed geographically isolated, and in consequence the companionship and the day-to-day practical aid once given by the extended family is no longer available, clearly the socialisation process within the neighbourhood will become more important. Therefore, a brief examination of the previous work concerning the relationship between the elementary and extended families is a necessary corollary to a discussion of the neighbourhood situation of the elementary family.

The terminology of these arguments has often been vague, with the result that the precise meaning of their conclusions has sometimes been lost. In this discussion, the 'extended family' will refer to 'any persistent kinship grouping of persons related by descent, marriage, or adoption, which is wider than the elementary family in that it characteristically spans three generations from grandparents to grandchildren'.[1] This is something of a mouthful but it is always necessary to define fully if results are to have a general applicability.

The relationship between the elementary and extended families in the American context, was discussed by Talcott Parsons 20 years ago. In his analysis of the social structure of the family, he concluded: '. . . structural analysis clearly shows that, if the u.s. is to remain and develop further as a democratic, urbanised, industrialised society, with a large measure of equality of opportunity, the range of possible family structures which are compatible with this type of society is very narrow.'[2] He further asserted that the isolation of the elementary family is a functional prerequisite in modern society.

This argument was supported by Linton. Analysing the current predicament of the family, Linton commented: 'The outstanding feature of this situation is the almost complete breakdown of the consanguine (extended) family as a functional unit. Although the Western European consanguine grouping has never dominated the conjugal (elementary) one, its potentialities for functioning and its claims on the individual were much stronger a hundred years ago than they are today. This breakdown seems to be directly correlated with the increased opportunities for both spatial and social mobility which have been created by the current technological revolution.'[3] He suggested that the extended family retains its functions only when the advantages of doing so outweigh the disadvantages, such as in the few capitalist dynasties that remain or in the long-settled rural areas. This questioning of the importance of the

---

[1] Rosser and Harris derived this definition after scrutinising the meaning and usage of terms employed in many studies of the family (C. Rosser and C. C. Harris, *The Family and Social Change*, Routledge, 1965, pp. 29–32).

[2] T. Parsons, 'The Social Structure of the Family', in R. N. Anshen, *The Family: its Functions and Destiny*, Harper Bros, 1949, p. 273.

[3] R. Linton, 'The Natural History of the Family', *ibid.*, p. 45.

contemporary extended family as a functioning unit led Litwak to examine more closely what function if any, the extended family currently fulfils. Unlike Parsons, Litwak supported his arguments by empirical evidence. He believed that Parsons had only been dealing with the 'classical extended family', characterised by geographical propinquity, occupational involvement and nepotism, and operating within a hierarchical authority structure. This he agreed, would certainly obstruct the operation of a system based on equality of opportunity. However, he claimed that a modified form of the extended family could be functional in contemporary industrial society. He defined this modified form as a series of elementary families 'bound together on an equalitarian basis with a strong emphasis on the extended family bonds as an end value'. It could be functional by providing significant and continuing aid to the elementary family. Such aid might, for example, be in the form of financial support given by parents to an adult son in the initial stages of his career. Since this type of economic assistance, Litwak argued, is only concerned with the standard of living and not with the occupational structure, it could not hinder mobility based on merit.[1] Furthermore, geographical mobility would be legitimised by the modified extended family, precisely because it is necessary for the occupational success that it desires for its members. Moreover, he saw no reason why physical separation should be incompatible with the modern extended family, for 'modern advances in communication techniques have minimised the socially disruptive effects of geographical distance'. On the basis of the data obtained from 920 housewives in Buffalo, New York, Litwak concluded, 'The modified extended family seems to be uniquely suited to provide succour in periods of movement'.[2]

An important qualification that must be made in respect of both the Parsonian and Litwakian theses, is that they both refer to a particular stratum of society. Parsons suggested that extended family relations are antithetical to democratic society

---

[1] E. Litwak, 'Occupational Mobility and Extended Family Cohesion', *Am. Sociol. Rev.*, vol. 25, no. 1 (Feb. 1960) pp. 9–13.

[2] E. Litwak, 'Geographical Mobility and Extended Family Cohesion', *Am. Sociol. Rev.*, vol. 25, no. 3 (June 1960), pp. 385–94.

'particularly under urban middle class conditions',[1] and Litwak's findings applied only to bureaucratic occupations.[2]

In turning to a consideration of British family life, it would, therefore, seem advisable to pay particular attention to the social class of the families that have been studied. Thus, in order to assess the relative influence of geographical mobility and social class on the functioning of the modern British extended family, the discussion that follows will be under four headings: first, immobile working-class families; second, mobile working-class families; third, immobile middle-class families; fourth, mobile middle-class families.

It is difficult to derive a universally understood definition of geographical mobility. This is because the concept of distance, which is inherent in the idea of mobility, is highly subjective. Its meaning tends to vary from one person to another and from social class to social class, depending on the means that are available of overcoming distance. It was hoped to meet this difficulty by adopting the following definition: an elementary family was deemed to have been geographically mobile when it had moved so far from its extended family that a visit to them presented 'considerable difficulty'; the need to prearrange the visit constituting 'considerable difficulty'.

IMMOBILE WORKING-CLASS FAMILIES

The British accounts of working-class family life which appeared during the 1950s suggested that perhaps the 'classical extended family' in which geographical propinquity, occupational involvement and nepotism played a significant role, had its contemporary manifestations. It is important to include here a description of the family life revealed in these studies, in order to understand the impact that geographical mobility had on such families.

Bethnal Green was a typical 'traditional' working-class area, characterised as it was by low population turnover, high-density housing and little opportunity for occupational advancement. In their investigation there Young and Willmott found a

---

[1] T. Parsons, 'A Revised Analytical Approach to the Theory of Social Stratification', in R. Bendix and S. M. Lipset, *Class, Status and Power*, Free Press of Glencoe, 1953, p. 116.

[2] Litwak, *op. cit.*, p. 394.

close-knit network of kin.[1] Regular contact between members of the extended family, particularly between mother and married daughters, was made possible by close residential proximity. Associated with this regular contact, was a reciprocal aid system. The extended family provided its members with both sociability and assistance, on a daily domestic basis as well as in personal crises. In this situation, there was no necessity for people to call upon neighbours for help except in emergencies. Indeed, the conditions of cramped living and the associated fears of intrusiveness mitigated against the development of intensive relationships outside the family.

It was the poor housing conditions mentioned above, that precipitated the demolition of property by the L.C.C. and the 'enforced' movement of some of the East-enders to the housing estates on the fringe of London. The changes for the family which such a move wrought, will be discussed in the next section.

MOBILE WORKING-CLASS FAMILIES

Working-class families who have been voluntarily mobile have seldom been studied systematically in Britain. Rather, the emphasis has been placed on the working-class families who have been moved involuntarily in response to redevelopment. During their investigations of such populations, somewhat similar family patterns were found by Mogey at Barton,[2] and by Young and Willmott at 'Greenleigh'. For example, Young and Willmott discovered that the effect of moving Bethnal Green inhabitants out to 'Greenleigh' was to disrupt much of the old-style family life. They reported that the amount of social contact with kin was drastically reduced,[3] because the physical distance between the new estate and Central London necessitated a long, and often prohibitively expensive, journey. As a result, when visits did occur they had to be prearranged. This introduced into the family relationship an element of formality that could never have existed in the close-knit network of the old area. Mrs Harper, one of the 'Greenleigh' respondents, contrasted the old

[1] M. Young and P. Willmott, *Family and Kinship in East London*, Penguin, 1965 (first pub. 1957), pp. 44–61. See also J. Klein, *Samples from English Cultures*, vol. 1, Routledge, 1965, pp. 123–39.

[2] J. M. Mogey, *Family and Neighbourhood*, Oxford University Press, 1956, pp. 77–97.

[3] *op. cit.*, pp. 131–3.

B

and the new situation. In Bethnal Green, she had led the life of the traditional extended family. 'All my family lived round Denby Street, and we were always in and out of each other's houses', she said. After her move, she complained of only being able to return to Bethnal Green five or six times a year when one of her elder sisters arranged a family party.

The natural consequence of this curtailment of social contacts, was a change in the role of the extended family. Neither in day-to-day affairs, nor even in emergencies such as the illness of the wife, could the elementary family rely on the assistance of relations. It became self-sufficient, with husbands or elder children performing the domestic tasks if the wife was indisposed. Even in these personal crises, there was little or no recourse to neighbours. Indeed, Young and Willmott wrote that, 'Even when neighbours were willing to assist, people were apparently reluctant to depend on them too much or confide in them too freely.'[1] This general unwillingness to assign to others the functions once fulfilled by kin, coupled with the fact that mobility was not undertaken voluntarily, prompts one to ask whether this change in the relationship between the elementary and extended families was a permanent one, or whether it was one consequence of rehousing that time would adjust. There is some evidence that it was indeed a temporary phenomenon. After only two years on the estate, some respondents at 'Greenleigh' told of relations who had joined them there.[2] One can deduce something of the likely long-term effect on family life, from the situation at Dagenham after 40 years. As Klein suggested, such an analogy must be drawn cautiously, for Dagenham had passed through its initial period of adjustment before the far-reaching social changes of conscription and war, affluence and the mass media, had been felt.[3]

Willmott's account of family life in Dagenham[4] tends to

---

[1] *op. cit.*, p. 142.
[2] *ibid.*, p. 134.
[3] Klein, *op. cit.*, pp. 221–2.
[4] P. Willmott, *The Evolution of a Community*, Routledge, 1963. Willmott made this study in the late 1950s, when Dagenham had been in existence for 30–40 years and had, therefore, had time to reach some level of stability. He was able to compare life at Dagenham in its formative years with life there in the 1950s, because two studies had already been made there, one by T. Young in 1934 and the other by Mass Observation in 1941–2.

indicate that the 'Greenleigh' phenomenon was indeed part of a transient phase, and by the second generation, for many families, the traditional pattern of the Bethnal-Green-type had re-emerged. However, in the light of the present discussion, the Dagenham families that did not conform to this pattern of frequent social contact and the related mutual rights and duties, claim attention. These were not only the young people who had moved into Dagenham from elsewhere, but also, parents whose children had moved away from the district.[1] The motivation for the outward migration of these children is interesting. While some had moved against their will in response to the housing shortage,[2] others had left voluntarily because they had 'moved up in the world';[3] in other words, they had been socially, as well as geographically mobile.

This would suggest, that a permanent change in the relationship between the working-class elementary and extended families, occurs when the physical mobility of the elementary family is voluntary.

IMMOBILE MIDDLE-CLASS FAMILIES

The few sociological descriptions of middle-class family life in Britain which do exist, tend to be concerned with the less mobile sector of the middle class. In this section, reference will be made to the work of Gavron, who studied two samples of young mothers in London. While one of her samples was of working-class respondents, the other was a middle-class one. The other sources are Rosser and Harris's investigation of family life in Swansea, and Willmott and Young's study in Woodford in which approximately two-thirds of their sample was middle-class. A direct comparison of the work of these authors is impeded by their different methods of data-tabulation, but their results all confirm certain trends.

It can be seen from Table 1 that the middle-class families lived further from their kin than the working-class samples with which they were compared.[4]

[1] Willmott, *op. cit.*, p. 36.
[2] *ibid.*, pp. 49–50.
[3] *ibid.*, p. 57.
[4] H. Gavron, *The Captive Wife*, Routledge, 1966, pp. 88, 94; Rosser and Harris, *op. cit.*, p. 213; P. Willmott and M. Young, *Family and Class in a London Suburb*, Routledge, 1960, p. 78.

TABLE I *The proximity of the parents of middle-class and working-class couples*

Location of Parents	Middle Class			Working Class		
	Woodford %	Swansea %*	London %*	Woodford %	Swansea %*	London %*
Same district	26	63	31†	42	85	51†
Elsewhere	74	37	69	58	15	49
TOTAL	100	100	100	100	100	100

* Refers to the wife's parents only
† Within a radius of one mile

Nevertheless, a surprisingly high proportion of the middle class couples lived near enough to their parents to make frequent visiting possible. The actual amount of contact with the extended family was discovered to be even greater than the statistics of location might suggest. Direct comparison between the various sources is difficult, for while Gavron tabulated the normal level of interaction, Rosser and Harris tabulated the accomplished visiting. However, their data (See Table 2) clearly indicate a class-differential, with the middle-class respondents seeing less of their kin than the working-class ones.[1] Nevertheless, the authors did find an appreciable amount of extended family visiting in the middle-class group.

It would appear from the Woodford data, that self-ascribed social class also plays a significant role in determining visiting levels. Willmott and Young found that while 32 % of the manual workers who regarded themselves as working-class had been visited by a relation in the last 24 hours, the equivalent figure for the manual workers who classified themselves as middle-class was only 22 %.[2]

Thus, these studies have shown that in their middle-class samples, there was a considerable amount of contact between the elementary and extended families. Even if relatives were not close enough to give daily aid, they were within reach should crises occur.

MOBILE MIDDLE-CLASS FAMILIES
There was no indication that the middle-class samples in the

[1] Gavron, *op. cit.*, pp.89–90; Rosser and Harris, *op. cit.*, p. 220.
[2] Willmott and Young, *op. cit.*, p. 116.

TABLE 2   *The frequency of contact between the wife and her mother in the Swansea and London samples*

Swansea

Frequency of contact	Middle class %	Working class %
In last 24 hours	44	56
24 hours – 1 week ago	32	27
More than 1 week ago	24	17
TOTAL	100	100

London*

Frequency of contact	Middle class %	Working class %
Every day	3	15
More than once a week	17	35
Once a week	15	4
Irregularly	63	44
TOTAL	100	100

* Much of this data was derived by calculation from the limited amount of information given by Gavron. This explains why the total is not exactly 100%.

three studies mentioned above, contained what Musgrove has called the 'migratory elite'[1] or Susser and Watson, the 'spiralists'; in other words, those persons whose career patterns, *ipso facto*, imply geographical mobility. These 'spiralists' are the members of the new professions – the scientific, technical and administrative ones – for whom mobility in status and responsibility is through the status-hierarchies of the large-scale organisations and for whom social mobility 'is often accompanied by residential movement'.[2] One suspects that such people were seldom in evidence in Woodford. Willmott and Young admitted that the Woodford area was 'almost entirely without what many people would think of as the "upper" or "upper middle"

[1] F. Musgrove, *The Migratory Elite*, Heinemann, 1963.
[2] M. Susser and A. Watson, *Sociology in Medicine*, Oxford University Press, 1962, pp. 135–40.

class. The professions are represented by people like bank-managers, accountants and surveyors and such company-directors as live there work far more often in small (mainly family) concerns than in large-scale public companies. They (the Woodford professionals) seemed to us, in the course of interviewing, to have lives not sharply different from those of the other white-collar workers – the bank-clerks, insurance-agents, shop-keepers . . . who appeared so often on the interview schedules.'[1] Gavron's sample, too, although it contained proportionately more professionals and business-men than Willmott and Young's,[2] appeared to consist largely of immobile respondents. 79 % of the husbands of her middle-class samples were Londoners by birth.[3] In spite of their 'spiralist-type' occupations, their geographical immobility would appear to distinguish them from Susser and Watson's ideal-type. Their atypicality was probably attributable to the fact that they lived in the capital city, which, offering an abundance of job opportunities, facilitates social without geographical mobility.

Therefore, if the effect of geographical mobility on the functioning of the extended family is to be fully understood, it will be necessary to consider those members of the middle class who can unambiguously be regarded as 'mobile'. However, the family life of such people had not been studied systematically when this research was in its formative stage.[4] This being so, it was only possible to assume that if these mobile people were indeed 'isolate' and far-removed from their extended family, there would be no conflict between their loyalty to their relations and to their new community, regardless of the function that their extended family fulfilled.

As stated earlier, to study the socialisation-process at the

[1] Willmott and Young, *op. cit.*, p. xii.

[2] Gavron, *op. cit.*, p. 47.

[3] *ibid.*, p. 45.

[4] Bell has since published the findings of a study of mobile middle-class families living in Swansea. His work confirms the suggestions made by Litwak and others in America, that where social contact between kin is reduced to once or twice a year, the extended family can still fulfil a real and meaningful function by providing status-support to the young couple at that point in the husband's career when his income is at its lowest (C. Bell, 'Mobility and the Middle Class Extended Family', *Sociology*, vol. 2, no. 2 (May 1968), p. 173; See also his *Middle Class Families*, Routledge, 1968, pp. 87–96.

neighbourhood level, the sociologist ideally needs to find people with no existing ties in the new residential district. Under such circumstances these people would be more likely to turn to the neighbourhood for the companionship and the day-to-day assistance traditionally provided by kin. The foregoing analysis of the role of the extended family in contemporary Britain has revealed what kind of people are isolated from their kin. They are the geographically mobile members of the population. These people do not belong to a particular social class nor are they the people who make a once-and-for-all move as part of redevelopment schemes. Rather, they are the individuals for whom geographical mobility is an acknowledged and necessary feature of the work situation. Even where there is a strong emotional commitment to the extended family, contact between the geographically mobile elementary family and its extended family is infrequent. Thus such affective ties would seem unlikely to interfere with the development of non-familial relationships. It was felt that a chance agglomeration of geographically mobile families could be located most easily on new owner-occupied housing estates.

The aim of the research

The object of this research was to study over time the way in which friendship patterns develop amongst housewives on new housing estates. This friendship development would be related to two groups of potentially influential variables; characteristics of the physical environment and characteristics of the housewives themselves. This work would involve some repetition of previous research in the field, but this repetition would be deliberate. It was hoped that by using operational definitions for such terms as 'friend' and 'visit', a more rigorous manipulation of data could be arranged than hitherto.

The housewife was chosen as the unit of study for three reasons. First, the fact that the housewife tends to spend more time than her husband on the housing estate allows her more opportunity for making friends there. Second, unlike her husband, the housewife, particularly if she is also a mother of young children, may be largely confined to the estate. If she is unable to make social contacts elsewhere, the socialisation process in the immediate locality is likely to be more urgent and exacting for her. Third, there was the practical requirement that each estate population should be spoken with in the shortest possible period. Such a task would be eased if at least some of the interviews could be conducted in the daytime, as they could if the housewife only was to be seen.

Previous research

Homans has claimed that any small group can be characterised by four dimensions. These are the motives for joining the group, the activities of the group, the interaction between the members that the group activity generates, and the norms of the group.[1] Therefore, the first stage in any study of small groups in the extra-laboratory situation is to identify the group members and to measure the amount of interaction between them. In this investigation, visiting was chosen as the criterion of interaction. This choice was made for the following reason. Visiting requires effort and the physical involvement of the individual. In consequence, it is more likely to be impressed upon the memory than more casual forms of contact. Since the reliability of response in a study of this type is affected to a considerable degree by the ease of recall, this initial commitment to memory is important. Furthermore, the use of visiting as a criterion of interaction, removes the need to scale that elusive concept 'neighbourliness'.

Once the group members have been identified and the amount of interaction has been measured, the question of causality arises. To this end, it is necessary to establish what determines the development of interacting relationships – why A is attracted to B and C, rather than to say D and E – and also what factors determine the degree of interaction between them. Clearly there will, in some circumstances, be a relationship between these two sets of variables. For example, three individuals may have been attracted to each other because they all had small children. Once their friendship was established, their personal demands arising from the fact that they had small children, such as the need for babysitters or for advice on

<hr />

[1] G. C. Homans, *The Human Group*, Routledge, 1965 (first publ. 1951), pp. 81–107.

childish ailments, may intensify their interaction as they come to rely more and more on each other. However, for simplicity, these two dimensions of group life, the determinants of attraction and of interaction levels, will be considered separately.

THE DETERMINANTS OF ATTRACTION

Two factors have been shown to influence the composition of the neighbourhood group. These are the physical distance between the dwellings of the residents and the orientation of the dwellings to each other.[1]

The relationship between ecological factors and friendship formation was studied by Festinger, Schachter and Back on two housing projects, Westgate and Westgate West, for married veteran students at the Massachusetts Institute of Technology. They had hypothesised that friendship depended upon the extent of passive contacts. To this end, they showed that sociometric choices tended to be given to people living nearby, and that people living in end houses received fewer sociometric choices from their court neighbours than did the people living in the houses which faced into the court.[2]

Merton found a similar relationship between friendship formation and resident propinquity, in his study of the mutual home-ownership community of Craftown. He demonstrated the importance of the orientation of dwellings to the development of personal ties, by examining the data for 'across the street' friendships. He found that 74% of these friendships were between people both of whom lived in street-orientated dwellings; 22% were in cases where one of the friends lived in a street-orientated house; while only 4% were between people neither of whom lived in dwellings facing the street.[3]

However, both these studies were made among homogeneous populations. Festinger and his colleagues recognised the possible shortcoming of this fact when they stated, '. . . the people living

---

[1] L. Festinger, S. Schachter and K. Back, *Social Pressures in Informal Groups*, Tavistock, 1963 (first publ. 1950), pp. 33–59; R. K. Merton, 'The Social Psychology of housing', in W. Dennis *et al.*, *Current Trends in Social Psychology*, Pittsburgh University Press, 1951, pp. 163–217.

[2] Festinger *et al.*, *op. cit.*, pp. 33–59.

[3] Merton, *op. cit.*, pp. 163–217.

in these projects are highly homogeneous along the dimensions of occupation, age, class and family background, education, interests, aspirations and attitudes towards the community in which they lived.'[1] 'Whether these ecological factors would be as effective in more heterogeneous communities is, of course, a question for further empirical study. It seems likely that in such communities, ecological factors will play some part, though a less important one, in determining sociometric structure.'[2] Clearly, there is a need to investigate the process of friendship formation on housing estates that are not homogeneous along the dimensions of occupation, age, etc., and this is the intention of this study.

In the light of the work that has been discussed above, the following working hypotheses were derived for testing on socially heterogeneous housing estates:

Hypothesis 1: 'The development of visiting relationships depends upon physical distance.'

Hypothesis 2: 'The development of visiting relationships depends upon the position and orientation of dwellings.'

THE DETERMINANTS OF INTERACTION LEVELS

We now turn from this discussion of the decisive factors in the formation of neighbourhood groups, to an examination of the known determinants of the interaction levels within such groups. The determinants of visiting levels appear to fall into two categories: first, certain characteristics of the participating individuals themselves; and second, critical aspects of the physical environment in which they 'operate'.

In surveying the literature to identify the influential individual characteristics, it was often difficult to distinguish between neighbourhood visiting and all visiting. However, this shortcoming was inconvenient rather than vital, because the earlier findings were to serve only as pointers in the formulation of working hypotheses; other variables were to be tested too. Those characteristics of individuals that have been shown to affect their visiting levels, are: age, life-stage, work situation, social

---

[1] Festinger *et al.*, *op. cit.*, p. 20.
[2] *ibid.*, pp. 58–9.

class, 'a general willingness to befriend neighbours', the expectation of future geographical mobility and the length of residence on the estate.

It would appear that the relationship between age and the amount of neighbourhood visiting has not been examined specifically. Willmott and Young found in Woodford that non-relations (other friends as well as neighbours) visited their respondents less often as the age of the respondents increased.[1] Hodges and Smith related age, together with life-stage, to another aspect of neighbourhood behaviour – the dependence on the neighbourhood as a source of friends. They suggested that this dependence rises markedly with the birth of children and declines thereafter with increasing age.[2] Although no finding could be traced that related either the number or the age of children to the activity of the mother, there is some evidence that the possession of children provided the opportunity for the development of relationships. Bracey, in his comparison of family life on new estates in England and America, found that, 'The needs for advice or help with the children led to introductions and subsequently to greater friendliness on both sides of the Atlantic. . . . In England, small children are encouraged to bring their play-mates into the backgarden to play and this makes for friendly intercourse between mothers of young children.'[3] These findings suggest that a systematic examination was needed of the influence that both the age, and the life-stage, of the housewife exerts on her neighbourhood activity level. Accordingly, the following hypotheses were advanced:

Hypothesis 3: 'The individual level of within-estate visiting depends upon age.'

Hypothesis 4: 'The individual level of within-estate visiting depends upon the possession of young children.'

Allied to this consideration of the effect of age and children, is the effect of the housewife's work-situation on her visiting level. There is obviously some relationship between the possession of young children and the mother's employment, but no

---

[1] *op. cit.*, p. 107.

[2] M. W. Hodges and C. S. Smith, 'The Sheffield Estate', in *Neighbourhood and Community*, Social Research Series, Liverpool University Press, 1954, p. 111.

[3] H. E. Bracey, *Neighbours*, Routledge, 1964, pp. 118–9.

one could claim that it is a predictable one.[1] Willmott found at Dagenham that fewer of the wives who went out to work had received a visit from a non-relation in the past 24 hours compared with wives who were at home all day, although the difference was only small (34 % of wives working full-time, compared with 24 % of non-working wives).[2] Here again, there was a failure to distinguish between neighbourhood and other visiting, but nevertheless the effect of the housewife's work situation would seem worth investigating in the specific context of the neighbourhood. With this in mind, a testable hypothesis appeared to be:

Hypothesis 5: 'The individual level of within-estate visiting depends upon the work-situation.'

The influence of social class on visiting was considerered by Willmott and Young. The class differential that they discovered at Woodford, where 42 % of their middle-class respondents compared with 34 % of the working-class had been visited by a non-relation in the past 24 hours,[3] was also apparent at Dagenham.[4] Again, there was no distinction made between neighbourhood and other visiting. However, elsewhere in these works it is reported that both the working- and middle-class respondents tended to regard the neighbourhood as their source of friends. It would seem reasonable to conclude that a social class gradient exists with respect to neighbourhood visiting.

The reference above to the source of friends, introduces the

---

[1] For example, Viola Klein found in 1957 that one-sixth of the working wives in her sample were mothers of at least one child under school age. She produced the table below from data supplied by employers. It shows the proportion of married-

Mothers of children	Full-time workers		Part-time workers	
	no.	%	no.	%
under school-age	461	7·4	247	14·9
of school-age	1755	28·3	720	43·6

women workers who have young children. See V. Klein, *Britain's Married Women Workers*, Routledge, 1965, pp. 55–7.

[2] Willmott, *op. cit.*, pp. 60–1.

[3] Willmott and Young, *op. cit.*, p. 109.

[4] *ibid.*, p. 136. At Dagenham the proportion of respondents by social class, who had been visited by a friend in the previous 24 hours, was: 43% of the white-collar workers, 30% of the skilled, 27% of the semi-skilled, and 25% of the unskilled manual workers.

whole question of the willingness to befriend neighbours. There appear to be two elements to this – the general willingness to make friends of any kind and the willingness to seek one's friends amongst the neighbours. Bott suggested that the families who were highly geographically mobile and who were part of very loose-knit networks, were unwilling to make social overtures to their neighbours. This reluctance was explained by their belief that because they differed in significant respects from their neighbours, friendship based on mutual compatability and similar interests would be impossible with them.[1] Such people were not necessarily socially reserved, but rather their friendships were made outside the neighbourhood. This confirms Rossi's findings in his American study of the social psychology of urban residential mobility. Three of his conclusions are relevant in this context. First, the more mobile the area, the greater was the difference perceived to be (with respect to social class) between the residents themselves and their neighbours. Second, the more mobile the area, the more unfriendly was the neighbourhood perceived to be. Third, the more mobile the neighbourhood, the less likely were its residents to form personal ties with their neighbours. On the other hand, a further conclusion relating to socio-economic status indicated that 'the higher the status of a person, the more likely he is to enter into personal ties with others . . . through cultivating friendships'.[2] Since other writers have shown a positive correlation between socio-economic status and geographical mobility,[3] it would appear that the more mobile people, when they are also of high socio-economic status, are less likely to seek their social life in the neighbourhood, but are nevertheless, socially aggressive. It may be that the evident conflict between the findings of Rossi on the one hand, and Willmott and Young on the other, is attributable to the fact that the people who were studied in Woodford anticipated fewer physical moves in the

[1] E. Bott, *Family and Social Network*, Tavistock, 1968 (first publ. 1957), pp. 74–9. See also J. Klein, *op. cit.*, pp. 343–7.
[2] P. H. Rossi, *Why Families Move: a Study in the Social Psychology of Urban Residential Mobility*, Free Press of Glencoe, 1955, p. 39.
[3] See, e.g., D. Friedlander and R. J. Roshier, 'Internal Migration in England and Wales, Part II.: Recent Internal Migrants—their Movements and Characteristics', *Population Studies*, vol. 20, no. 1 (July 1966), pp. 50–1. For further references see Musgrove, *op. cit.*, pp. 46–9.

future, than Rossi's American sample. As Bracey has pointed out, the tendency is towards greater geographical mobility in the U.S. compared with Britain.[1]

This discussion has indicated the importance of studying the effect of both social class and geographical mobility on the amount of neighbourhood visiting in which the individual participates. Accordingly, the following working hypotheses were drawn up:

Hypothesis 6: 'The individual level of within-estate visiting depends upon socio-economic status.'

Hypothesis 7: 'The individual level of within-estate visiting depends upon past mobility behaviour.'

Hypothesis 8: 'The individual level of within-estate visiting depends upon the expectation of future mobility.'

In order to elucidate upon the effect of the willingness to befriend neighbours, a further hypothesis was developed:

Hypothesis 9: 'The individual level of within-estate visiting depends upon the attitude of the individual to a new neighbour.'[2]

In response to Bott's suggestion that some people deliberately cultivate friendships elsewhere in preference to neighbourhood ones, it was also necessary to establish whether the amount of visiting to friends living off the estate, influenced the level of visiting on the estate. Thus it was planned to test the following hypothesis:

Hypothesis 10: 'The individual level of within-estate visiting depends upon the number of visits to friends elsewhere.'

Although it was hoped to find respondents whose relations were not living locally, the possibility of having local kin could not be overlooked. This was particularly important in view of the fact that Fellin and Litwak had found that the presence of relations in the residential area was detrimental to neighbourhood integration.[3] Therefore the following hypothesis was formulated:

---

[1] *op. cit.*, pp. 16–27.

[2] The form of this measure was suggested by P. Fellin and E. Litwak, 'Neighbourhood Cohesion under Conditions of Mobility', *Am. Sociol. Rev.*, vol. 28, no. 3 (June 1963), p. 373.

[3] *ibid.*, p. 375.

Hypothesis 11: 'The individual level of within-estate visiting depends upon the number of visits made to relations.'

It will be noticed that the last two hypotheses refer to the number of visits made to non-estate friends and relations, rather than to the location of such persons. Whilst it was proposed to obtain data on their location, it was considered too difficult to derive for each respondent some composite measure of distance for what would, in all probability, be varying numbers of persons. It was felt that the number of visits that the individual housewife made to these external groups of friends and relations, would provide a good estimate of her commitment to off-the-estate relationships.

Although no reference was found in the literature relating neighbourhood visiting behaviour to the possession of a car, a number of sources stress the facility that a car offers, of maintaining relationships at a distance from the residential area.[1] It was felt that the wife of a two-car family would be at a distinct advantage in this respect. Therefore, a further hypothesis was drawn up:

Hypothesis 12: 'The individual level of within-estate visiting depends upon the number of cars in the household.'

Fellin and Litwak, while not referring specifically to the amount of neighbourhood visiting, found that there was a positive relationship between the development of neighbourhood friendships and affiliation with voluntary associations.[2] They suggested that membership of such associations offered an opportunity to initiate friendships. In response to their reasoning, it was thought worthwhile to test the hypothesis:

Hypothesis 13: 'The individual level of within-estate visiting depends upon the number of social clubs to which the individual belongs' (restricting the clubs to those where it might be feasible to meet other estate members).

Having discussed at some length those characteristics of the individual that influence her activity level within the neighbourhood group, it is expedient to consider the second category of

[1] See, e.g., J. Klein, *op. cit.*, p. 332.
[2] *op. cit.*, pp. 375–6.

activity determinants. These are the aspects of the physical environment in which the social group operates.

It will be recalled that in a homogeneous population, Festinger and his colleagues, and Merton found that friendships develop on the basis of proximity and dwelling orientation. Whyte, in his study of the social-life of Park Forest residents, found that these factors influenced not only the formation of friendships but the activity level within such friendships, too. Whyte concluded that the 'areas with high partying records usually prove to be the ones with the layout best adapted to providing the close-knit neighbourly group. . . .'[1] Such layouts tended to consist of a cluster of inner-orientated houses[2] or, in British terms, of cul-de-sacs. While Whyte's study was not a very rigorous one, there appeared to be no British findings which either confirmed or rejected his conclusion on the relationship between the site-plan and activity rates.[3] British workers had dealt with rather different concepts in relation to spatial layouts. For example, Willmott found at Dagenham that there was a greater feeling of friendliness in the cul-de-sacs compared with the less intimate groupings of houses.[4] Kuper, in discussing the cohesion of the neighbourhood groups at Braydon Road, Coventry, admitted that cul-de-sacs offered better opportunities for contact, but suggested that their very intimacy could give rise to conflict and insecurity.[5]

The somewhat inconclusive nature of this work on the relationship between social activity and site-plans, was justification in itself for examining the whole question in this study. However, there was an even stronger inducement to do so. By

---

[1] W. H. Whyte, *The Organization Man*, Penguin, 1960 (first publ. 1956), p. 307.
[2] *ibid.*, pp. 314–20.
[3] Barbara Kuper has published a short study *Privacy and Private Housing* (1968) sponsored by architectural and building bodies, in which she explored this relationship on two private estates. Although her estate populations were 'homogeneous' she concluded that 'on the one estate the cluster design seems actually to have worked against contact, and on the other the cluster appeared to be immensely successful'. However, her assumption of homogeneity appeared to be ill-founded and she admitted herself that individual characteristics, which she made no attempt to control, may have distorted her conclusions.
[4] Willmott, *op. cit.*, pp. 77–83.
[5] L. Kuper, 'Blueprint for Living Together', in L. Kuper (ed.), *Living in Towns*, Cresset, 1953, pp. 117, 150.

developing new layouts of the Radburn-type, architects and planners appear to be perpetuating the myth that what the public wants are the cosy groupings of houses that in the past have been manifested in the cul-de-sacs. Somehow they have become convinced that such intimate formations are desirable because they promote a healthy social life.[1] Clearly it was essential to test their assumption using a rigorous analytical approach. Accordingly, the following working hypothesis which was to be the core of the whole study, was formulated:

Hypothesis 14: 'The amount of within-estate visiting depends upon the site-plan.'

It should be mentioned that the site-plan was not the only feature of the residential environment whose influence was to be examined. There were others, but they will be discussed later because they did not arise directly from earlier research but were original to this work.

A discussion of the influence that the age of the residential community exerts on the behaviour of its occupants, has deliberately been postponed until this juncture. The reason for this is that it is difficult to categorise this variable either as an aspect of the environment, or as an individual characteristic. It belongs to the first category in the sense that the rate of the development of an estate is beyond the control of the individual resident and being extraneous to him or her, could be classified as an environmental factor. On the other hand, it could be placed in the second category if one argues that each family arrived on the estate at a different time, and thus the duration of residence is specific to each family. It will be seen in the next chapter how the design of this study accommodated both of these viewpoints. For the present, it will be sufficient to outline Mogey's conclusions on the influence of the age of the estate. He has suggested that every new neighbourhood passes through two, or possibly three phases. The first phase, occupying the

---

[1] The relationship between the physical environment and social life has been discussed on many occasions in planning journals. See, e.g., I. Rosow, 'The Social Effects of the Physical Environment', *J. Am. Inst. Planners*, vol. 27, no. 2 (May 1961), pp. 127–33, and *ibid.*, H. J. Gans 'Planning and Social Life', pp. 134–40. A British example is M. Broady 'Social Change and Town Development', *Town Planning Rev.*, vol. 36, no. 4 (Jan. 1966), pp. 269–78.

C

early months when gardens and roads are unmade, is characterised by 'friendliness, intense interaction in small groups, and the continuous sharing of equipment and news. . . .'[1] In the second phase, a contraction occurs from the relationships based on common problems, and 'contact tends to become restricted to the immediate neighbours'.[2] It is possible that a third phase exists in which 'equilibrium is reached between these two extremes'.[3] It will be appreciated that Mogey was dealing with two aspects of group life which change over time. He was dealing with both the membership of the social groups and the level of interaction within these groups. Furthermore, he was not being very precise in either respect. This study aimed to show how the duration of residence affected both of these factors.

There have been indications in the course of this discussion, of the ways in which earlier work gave rise to the working hypotheses for this research. It was proposed to remedy some of the shortcomings and omissions of this earlier research in two ways. First, the previous explanations of neighbourhood group-formation referred only to homogeneous neighbourhoods. It was hoped to discover whether the topographical factors that proved so important in the homogeneous neighbourhoods, still exerted a potent influence in heterogeneous ones. Second, it was clear that no comprehensive attempt had been made to explain activity levels within neighbourhood groups. In this work, it was planned to identify those characteristics both of the individual and of her physical environment which determine her visiting activity within the neighbourhood.

[1] R. N. Morris and J. Mogey, *The Sociology of Housing*, Routledge, 1965, p. 42. A detailed statement of the phase hypothesis appears in J. M. Mogey, 'Social Aspects of English Family Housing: from Poverty to Privacy', in N. Anderson (ed.), *Studies in the Family, III*, Göttingen: Vandenhoeck and Ruprecht, 1958.

[2] *ibid.*, p. 43.

[3] *ibid.*, p. 43.

2 The Research

The method

The proposed examination of the effect of environmental, or planning, variables on within-estate activity obviously demanded a careful comparison of the activity on estates which differed in significant respects. For example, when investigating the influence of the site-plan, it would be necessary to compare *the mean activity levels* on say a cul-de-sac and a linear development. However, such a comparison would be naive if no allowance was made for the composition of the estate populations. This is clearly so since the discussion in Chapter 1 revealed that certain personal characteristics affect individual, and hence estate, activity levels. Thus, if such comparisons were to be valid, some technique was required that would control the influence of the relevant characteristics of the individuals living on the estates. The procedure developed by Devereux in his study of community participation in the Springfield Rural Community, commended itself for this purpose.

Devereux obtained for each individual, a participation potential or 'the level at which he could be expected to participate, if participation were determined solely on the basis of these relevant characteristics'.[1]

This participation potential was predicted from a multiple regression formula.[2] This formula had been calculated by

[1] E. C. Devereux, 'Neighbourhood and Community Participation', *J. Soc. Issues*, vol. 16, no. 4 (1960), p. 68.

[2] See Statistical Glossary. It is suggested that the reader should at this stage read the Glossary right through unless he already has a working knowledge of elementary statistical method.

regressing participation on those 'relevant characteristics' of age, socio-economic status and sex, which previous research had shown to be related to community participation. The participation potential of the neighbourhood was taken as the mean of the participation potentials of the residents. By comparing for each neighbourhood, its actual with its potential participation, it was possible to identify those neighbourhoods that were 'normal' and those that were higher or lower than 'normal' on participation.

By substituting 'within-estate visiting' for 'community participation' Devereux's method offered two distinct advantages for this research. The multiple regression operation itself would allow one to test the hypotheses concerning the determinants of individual visiting levels. It would not only indicate which variables were influential, but also the relative contribution which each variable made to the explanation of the individual visiting rate. Further, an assessment could be made of the effect of the planning variables on the overall estate activity level. This assessment could be accomplished in two stages. First, the individual, and thence the estate, activity potentials could be derived from the regression formula. If these potentials were then related to the actual activity levels, a mean value of activity deviance could be calculated for each estate. This figure would indicate whether each estate was 'normal' (i.e. its actual and its potential activity levels would be equal), or whether it was under- or over-achieving on activity (i.e. its actual activity would fall below or exceed its potential activity, respectively). Next, by relating the ranking of the estates on activity deviance to their ranking on specific planning variables, it would be possible to assess the degree of influence exerted by these planning characteristics on estate activity. For example, if as Whyte has suggested, the cul-de-sac is more conducive to high activity than the linear development, the estates with a cul-de-sac-type layout should over-achieve while the linear ones should under-achieve.

Thus the Devereux technique provided the facility for testing all the hypotheses relating to visiting levels, individual and estate. On this basis, it was decided to utilise it and the questionnaires were designed to extract the relevant type of information.

For the multiple regression analysis certain basic information was required from each of the estate housewives. It was necessary to know the total number of visits that she had made to other estate members within a given time-period. The previous month was taken as the relevant period, for it was believed that activity during that time was sufficiently recent to minimise memory-errors. At the same time, a month was thought to be long enough to offer the individual adequate scope for visiting. This total number of within-estate visits would act as the dependent variable in the regression model. In addition, it was essential to obtain information on those demographic and other individual characteristics, such as age or geographical mobility expectation, that would be required as the independent variables in the regression.

It will be noticed that the identity of the persons visited was irrelevant for the regression analysis. Rather, this information was required for the sociometric[1] analysis. It would be used to test the hypotheses concerning the formation of social groups, namely, the hypotheses that the development of visiting relationships depends upon both physical distance and the position and orientation of dwellings.

In order to satisfy the requirements of both the regression and sociometric analyses, it was important that all operational terms should be carefully defined. It was felt that the term 'neighbourhood', which had been employed frequently in past research to refer to the operational field, was too vague. It failed to circumscribe a specific area. In consequence, the term 'estate' was used during all interviews with residents. In order to ensure that the term 'estate' would be unambiguous, only estates that were clearly defined physically were included in the study. A 'visit' was taken as an 'occasion upon which one person actually enters the house of another'. It was hoped, thereby, to preclude casual contacts or such preliminaries to visiting as a call to extend the invitation. (To ensure that this distinction had been

---

[1] Sociometric Analysis means the analysis of a social group's choices, rejections, etc., within their own group. This usually takes a simple form. For example the members of a group may be asked to nominate the person(s) within the group who they would choose to accompany them on a holiday. The results are sometimes expressed by the drawing of a sociogram but are handled more effectively by a branch of mathematics known as matrix algebra (see Appendix VI).

understood by the respondent, the purpose of each visit was ascertained.)

Data collection

The data collection proceeded in the following manner. First, nine suitable estates were chosen, one for the pilot study,[1] the other eight for the main study. Second, the interview schedule A was tested on the pilot estate. The object of this first series of interviews was to obtain information on family characteristics, the move to the estate, any early estate social contacts and the reaction of new residents to other estate members. Third, using the pre-tested schedule (see Appendix I) each housewife on the selected estates was interviewed as soon as possible after her move into the new house. Fourth, one year later the second interview schedule, schedule B, requiring more detailed information about visiting behaviour, on and off the estate, was tested on the pilot population. (For final form of schedule B see Appendix I.) Fifth, the second round of interviews was completed on the study population. These processes will now be considered in more detail.

The estates

It was decided to confine this investigation to private housing estates. This decision was made for a number of reasons.

Private estates offered a better opportunity for the study of the 'nuclear family in isolation'. Only if the residents were complete strangers to each other and to the area, could one be sure of obtaining a true impression of the socialisation process. From the discussion in Chapter 1, it would appear that the people who are most likely to be free of existing family and friendship ties in the area of their new home, belong to the geographically mobile section of the population. It is unlikely that such families would be found on local authority estates.

---

[1] Before an actual survey is carried out in an unresearched topic, it is usual to carry out a pilot survey. The purpose of this is to test the questionnaire, i.e., to ascertain that the concepts and language used are meaningful, to find out if the question order is correct and the many other factors which if uncorrected could invalidate the main research study.

Municipal housing-allocation policies generally mitigate against short-stay residents. Furthermore, new local authority estates often consist of communities that have been moved en masse and therefore are not necessarily populated by strangers. The logical place to seek the mobile families then, was on private estates.

Moreover, the home-owning public seemed to be potentially more heterogeneous than the local authority tenant population. In order to assess the relative effects on the socialization process of such individual characteristics as age and social class, it was desirable to study a population that was heterogeneous along these dimensions. The Building Society statistics set out in Table 3 below, indicate the extent to which age does indeed vary amongst house-purchasers.

TABLE 3   *The distribution of building society borrowers by age*[1]

Age	% Borrowers
Under 25	14·96
25–34	42·02
35–44	24·67
45–54	15·84
55 and over	2·51
TOTAL	100·00

The discussion surrounding the 'embourgeoisement thesis' has revealed that home-ownership is by no means the exclusive domain of the middle class. Goldthorpe and Lockwood have pointed out that an affluent section of the manual working class is equalling and sometimes surpassing many white-collar families in standards of domestic living and in ownership of durable goods (including homes).[2] On this basis, it seemed reasonable

[1] Building Societies Association, 'Analysis of Home Loans made by Building Societies during October 1964', *Building Society Statistics*, no. 6 (special issue, Apr. 1965). See also R. Wilkinson, 'Building Society Statistics: A Review Article', *Urban Studies*, vol. 2, no. 2 (Nov. 1965), p. 190. While more recent statistics are available, the 1964 figures were the ones that related to the decision to study home-owners.

[2] J. H. Goldthorpe and D. Lockwood, 'Not so Bourgeois After All', *New Society*, vol. 1, no. 3 (18 Oct. 1962), pp. 18–19; see also 'Affluence and the British Class Structure', *Sociol. Rev.* (new ser.), vol. 11, no. 2 (1963), pp. 133–63.

to assume that there would be diversity of social class amongst owner-occupiers.

It is also the case that private estates have a greater variation of housing type than publicly-owned ones. The combination on one estate of dwellings of a different style and price, should offer greater scope for status differentiation, and hence be of more interest to the sociologist.

Further there has been a gross over-emphasis on the public sector in past housing research in this country. The preoccupation with research on local authority tenants seemed unjustifiable for the following reason. Between 1958 and 1966, when this research was commenced, the annual number of houses completed for the private sector exceeded the number for all other sectors combined (see Table 4).

TABLE 4   *Permanent houses completed: England and Wales*[1]

Year	Completed houses (000s)			% for Private Owners
	For private Owners	For local Authorities	Total	
1958	124	113	241	51·4
1959	146	99	249	58·7
1960	162	103	269	60·2
1961	170	93	269	63·4
1962	167	105	279	59·9
1963	168	97	271	62·2
1964	210	119	337	62·5
1965	206	133	347	59·4
1966	198	145	350	56·5

* This total applies to *all* houses completed and includes houses completed for housing associations, etc., in addition to those completed for private owners and local authorities.

Lastly, only comparatively small estates were required for the study and these were more readily available in the private sector. The reasons for this restriction in size will be discussed in the next section.

In order to test the hypotheses relating planning features to activity levels, it was necessary to have variation amongst the

[1] Source: Ministry of Housing Statistics. Abstracted from Table 56, p. 60, 'Permanent Houses Completed', *Annual Abstract of Statistics*, no. 103, 1966.

estates with respect to the site-plan, the degree of admixture of housing type and price, and size. An upper limit of 50 houses was imposed for four reasons. First, the respondent was to be asked to identify herself with the members of 'the estate'. Therefore, it was essential that its boundaries should be clearly defined and universally understood. This condition was more likely to be satisfied if the estate was small. Second, it was important from the methodological viewpoint that each respondent should have a realistic chance of coming into contact with every other estate member. Third, the restricted size would enable the authors, who alone were to be responsible for interviewing every housewife, to study a number of estates in the time available. Fourth, some questions were to be time-conditioned so it was important that all the estate members should be interviewed in the shortest possible period. Such a condition clearly demanded some limitation on estate size.

According to the initial research programme, the Stage 1 interviews were to be completed by a pre-arranged date. Therefore, only estates that would be completed and occupied by then, were acceptable. Furthermore, the period over which occupation took place, needed to be as short as possible so that all the estate members were passing through the 'settling-in' stage simultaneously.

With these pre-conditions in mind, some 58 estates were inspected in the North Midlands. Many estates were eliminated because their development period extended over several years rather than months, particularly in the case of the estates of very expensive houses. While the builders on the sites were able to estimate completion dates, naturally they were unable to guarantee that all the houses would either be sold, or occupied, by a given time. Nine estates were finally chosen for the investigation; eight of these were to be included in the main part of the study, the ninth was to be used for pilot work. The eight study estates will now be described. In each case the reader would be advised to refer to the appropriate site-plan (see Appendix II).

WHITMARSH[1]

Whitmarsh is a small textile town of some 17,500 people

[1] To preserve anonymity, new street and place names have been fabricated.

which is expanding to accommodate Manchester commuters.

The estate is approximately one mile from Whitmarsh town centre. It consists of two parallel cul-de-sacs, (running in a west–east direction), Dorchester Close and Uppingham Close and a third, Meadowside, which links the other two to the main road. All the 48 dwellings on the site are detached. There are seven two-bedroomed bungalows all lying on the southern side of Dorchester Close and 32 three-bedroomed houses interspersed with nine four-bedroomed houses. While the accommodation of all the three-bedroomed houses is the same, the frontage design is periodically reversed (see site-plan), so that the side entrances of adjacent houses are sometimes contiguous and sometimes remote. All the houses have a through living-room, with the kitchen to the side of it and at the rear of the house. The elevation of the site is such that the land falls away from the southern side of Dorchester Close, with the houses on the southern side of Uppingham Close situated in a trough. The result of this is that these Uppingham Close residents are overlooked both to the front and to the rear.

On the periphery of the estate are fields to the north and west, existing houses to the east and the main road cutting to the south.

ASTON

On the boundary of the pottery-manufacturing city of Stoke-on-Trent lies Jersey Close, Aston. This cul-de-sac was built between an existing road and a railway line. Its position provides easy access to the 'potbanks' (pottery factories) of Longton and to two large factories which between them have contributed significantly to the diversification of industry in Stoke-on-Trent.

The estate consists of one detached and 18 pairs of semi-detached, three-bedroomed houses. Although the houses on the south side of the Close are slightly higher than the ones on the north side, the absence of through-rooms makes it impossible for the residents to look straight through the houses opposite. The lounge is at the front of each house, with a dining-kitchen leading off it and running the width of the house at the rear.

HUNTLEY

The estate is an in-filling development between a main road

and a minor road in the Newcastle-u-Lyme R.D. Three pairs of semi-detached two-bedroomed bungalows and one detached bungalow, lie on the minor road (Pasture Lane) opposite local authority houses. The cul-de-sac, Oakham Close, lies parallel with Pasture Lane and consists of six pairs of semi-detached bungalows, similar to the ones on the minor road, and three detached bungalows. These two roads are linked by Hawthorn Road which contains three pairs of semi-detached houses and one detached one, all situated on the slightly elevated, eastern side of the road. Each dwelling on the site has a lounge overlooking the road, but whereas the kitchen is also at the front in the bungalows, it is at the rear in the houses.

GARTON

Garton is a town with a population of approximately 20,000 near to Stoke. It is made up of a number of separate communities that developed in the nineteenth century around the coalmines and quarries of the Potteries. The isolation of these settlements was reinforced by the tracts of derelict land that were left between them, as the mines became worked out. The segmented nature of Garton has been stressed here because of the identification with these small communities that was apparent among some of the respondents on the Garton estate.

In 1966, on a stretch of derelict land, both low-priced dwellings for owner-occupation, and local authority houses, were under construction. The unit selected for study, is a visually self-contained cul-de-sac, Hill Close. It consists of 17 semi-detached bungalows (the eighteenth bungalow to complete the odd pair, was nominally included in another road). It is situated on a steep incline such that the bungalows at the 'closed' end of the cul-de-sac are in the highest position with an uninterrupted view across a valley. All the bungalows, whether they have two or three bedrooms, have the living-room at the front and the kitchen at the side of the dwelling.

GRASMERE CLOSE, WIXLEY

Wixley is a light-manufacturing town of some 10,000 people in the centre of Staffordshire. It is gaining popularity as a residential area.

Grasmere Close is situated about one mile from the town centre. This cul-de-sac was built on the grounds of a large house, demolished to make way for the estate. The 12 high-priced dwellings which were individually designed, stand on generous plots, secluded from each other by mature trees.

SKILBECK

This is a short linear development of 9 houses on the Staffordshire–Cheshire boundary. As on the Grasmere Close estate, each plot was developed independently but the plots are smaller than the ones at Wixley, and the houses themselves, give a greater appearance of similarity. The houses back onto older ones from which the householders are not allowed to fence themselves off. Clearly, provision has been made for a road-widening scheme beyond the frontages, so movement between the houses is somewhat hampered by the absence of a pavement along the busy main road.

UTTING

Utting is a mining and industrial town of some 16,000 people in North Staffordshire. The town has a reputation for its individual character and independence, perhaps developed in response to its comparative geographical isolation, for it lies in a valley between two high ridges.

The small linear estate on Brook Lane lies half a mile to the north of the town centre. The eight dwellings were built on the land belonging to one of the householders. The site falls away steeply from Brook Lane to a stream. While there is an open aspect to the rear of the estate, there are older houses opposite at the front. The estate consists of six detached two-bedroomed bungalows and one pair of semi-bungalows, all built at a lower level than the road.

CHURCH CLOSE, WIXLEY

The second Wixley estate is a small horseshoe-shaped development of four pairs of semi-detached houses, lying close to the town centre between Church Street and the railway. Six of the houses are two-bedroomed with a through living-room and kitchen at the rear. The other two, have three bedrooms but a smaller living-room and a downstairs bathroom.

Recalling that these eight estates were selected primarily for their planning characteristics, Table 5 sets out those planning features of the estates that were considered to be potentially influential in determining estate activity levels. These features were the site layout, the size of the estate and the level and heterogeneity of house price.

TABLE 5   *Planning features of the estates – a summary*

Estate	Site-layout	No. dwellings on completed site	Approx. mean price of dwellings (£)	No. price groups
Whitmarsh	compact	48	4,000	3
Aston	cul-de-sac	37	2,820	2
Huntley	compact	29	2,630	3
Garton	cul-de-sac	17	2,410	2
Grasmere	cul-de-sac	12	7,200	7
Skilbeck	linear	9	5,610	2
Utting	linear	8	3,250	1
Church Close	cul-de-sac	8	3,000	1

Before proceeding to a description of the people who lived on these estates, it would seem advisable to consider the interview response.

The response

In order to interview each estate-member as soon as she took up residence, it proved necessary to make many and frequent visits to each estate. The situation was aggravated by the fact that the occupation period was longer than anticipated on most of the estates. The explanation for this lay in general financial conditions. In the summer of 1966 mortgages became very difficult to obtain, with the result that the rate at which the houses were sold on the selected estates was severely retarded.

A few houses on four of the eight estates, were still unoccupied in July 1966, by which time the Stage 1 interviews should have been completed. The inevitable outcome was that the Stage 1 visiting data was only of limited value, since it referred to incomplete populations. Although the interviewing period was prolonged to October, some houses still remained unoccupied and provision had to be made to extract Stage 1-type data from their eventual occupants at the Stage 11 interviews. Table 6 indicates the rate at which the estates were occupied.

When approached at the first interview, the majority of respondents showed great interest in the research. The task of eliciting a favourable response was doubtless facilitated by two factors. The potential respondents were currently battling with the problems inherent in new houses and were only too willing to relate their difficulties to an outsider. Moreover, many of them had been so preoccupied with straightening their new homes, that they had had neither the time nor the inclination to entertain their new neighbours. Such comments as, 'I'd be ashamed for anyone to see the house before the carpets are down', were frequently heard. Yet, because of this solitude, albeit self-imposed, these housewives were eager to talk to someone and an interview provided an ideal opportunity.

There was only one refusal out of 139 people who were approached during the first round of interviews. This person was on the Huntley estate. As no-one on the estate reported any contact with her, it was assumed that her refusal would not critically bias the results.

During the second round of interviews, the attitude of the respondents to the study was mixed. The majority expressed continuing friendly interest in it. However, a few were becoming a little suspicious and inhibited since they had not been expecting a follow-up interview. This was no oversight. It was felt that if the housewife had known in advance that her social activity was to fall under further scrutiny, there might have been a 'halo' effect, obscuring the true social situation.

Four of the original respondents were lost from the study population. Three of these had moved away. However, two of them had been replaced some months before the Stage 11 interviews so their replacements were interviewed and treated in the

TABLE 6 *The occupation pattern on the estates*

Estate	No. dwellings occupied by								
	July 65	*Sept. 65*	*Dec. 65*	*Mar. 66*	*June 66*	*Sept. 66*	*Dec. 66*	*Mar. 67*	*June 67*
Whitmarsh	—	—	—	1	11	24	37	45	47*
Aston	—	10	24	29	33	36*	36	36	36
Huntley	—	—	—	3	9	22	23	25	26*
Garton	—	—	—	—	5	13	15	16*	16
Grasmere	2	2	3	5	8	11	12*	12	12
Skilbeck	3	4	6	6	8	9*	9	9	9
Utting	—	2	5	6	6	6	8*	8	8
Church Close	—	—	—	—	5	8*	8	8	8
TOTAL	5	18	38	50	85	129	148	159	162

* For the purpose of this study, the estate was then regarded as 'completed'.

same way as the other new residents. The house that had belonged to the third mover, at 11 Jersey Close, Aston remained empty throughout the Stage II interview period. Therefore, this represented an irretrievable loss. The fourth of the original respondents to drop out of the study, was persistently absent from the estate, nursing a sick mother. In consequence she was never discovered at home, despite repeated call-backs. As this lady had effectively opted out of the social life of the Aston estate, for the purposes of this study, she was regarded as having left it.

There were 25 new residents at Stage II. They were approached with interview schedule B, plus a supplementary sheet to extract Stage I-type data on family characteristics, motivation for moving, etc. (see Appendix I). Amongst these 25, there was one refusal. This person lived next door to the original refuser at Huntley. Again, no-one else on the estate reported any contact with her, although to what extent she interacted with her next-door neighbour, is of course unknown. Even a follow-up letter explaining the purpose of the study and the importance of 100% response, failed to persuade her to co-operate.

In designing the questionnaires, care was taken to avoid any questions that might induce reticence or non-response in the estate members. (This explains, for instance, why age was estimated, rather than established from the respondents.) However, three people refused to answer some questions, but these were not crucial to the derivation of sociometric or regression data.

The response situation is summarised in Table 7. It will be seen from this, that the study population consisted finally of 158 individuals.

The people

Tables 8–14 present a general picture of the estate populations in terms of their demographic composition and of their mobility-experience and expectation. Each estate population will be considered briefly to indicate its general character and any distinctive features.

TABLE 7 *The Response*

Stage I Interviews

Estate	No. persons approached	No. non-respondents	No. cooperative respondents
Whitmarsh	28	—	28
Aston	36	—	36
Huntley	23	1	22
Garton	15	—	15
Grasmere	12	—	12
Skilbeck	9	—	9
Utting	8	—	8
Church Close	8	—	8
TOTAL	139	1	138

Stage II Interviews

Estate	No. persons approached	No. non-respondents	No. cooperative respondents			
			Old	New	Replacements	Total
Whitmarsh	47	—	28	19	—	47
Aston	35†	1	33	—	1	34
Huntley	25	1	22	2	—	24
Garton	16	—	14	1	1	16
Grasmere	12	—	12	—	—	12
Skilbeck	9	—	9	—	—	9
Utting	8	—	8	—	—	8
Church Close	8	—	8	—	—	8
TOTAL	160	2	134	22	2	158

† This excludes the old respondent who had left the estate without being replaced.

WHITMARSH

This estate was populated predominantly by young couples in the early stages of their married lives. (Approximately 75% of the housewives were estimated to be under 40 years of age.) Four elderly couples had moved onto the estate for their retirement and, with one exception, they lived in the bungalows on Dorchester Close. Of all the populations studied, the Whitmarsh

D

one probably contained the highest proportion of 'spiralists'. The 'typical' husband here was performing a job, say as an electronics engineer or a research chemist, for which he required lengthy, specialist training.

While only one housewife anticipated an early move off the estate, for many of the respondents geographical mobility was an accepted corollary of job mobility. (62 % of the Whitmarsh respondents said that a change in her husband's job would certainly be accompanied by a move; while for a further 15 %, a move under such circumstances was a possibility.) 49 % of the housewives said that they had moved from their previous homes because their husbands had changed jobs. Table 13 suggests the diversity of areas from which the Whitmarsh respondents had moved. Amongst the areas named, were counties as far apart as Cumberland and Essex. The orientation of about a third of the housewives was towards the Manchester conurbation, either because they had moved from that area and still maintained regular contact with friends there, or because they had relations living there whom they visited fairly often. For some of the residents, their move had been an attempt to escape from the urban life of Manchester to the rural life, as they perceived it, of Whitmarsh.

ASTON

The population of Jersey Close tended to fall into two categories. In the first category were the young, childless couples who moved into their house on, or soon after, marriage. The wife was working full-time, usually in one of the local 'potbanks', and her husband was usually in a skilled or semi-skilled manual job at either the Michelin or Simplex factory. In the second category were the older couples, again predominantly working-class, but this time with children. They had lived previously in rented accommodation and had moved to Jersey Close when, for their individual reasons, they had decided to purchase a house. In this group were the 10 wives who, although they had young children, managed to go out to work either full-time or part-time, because they had relations living nearby who would look after the children. (Only one mother on the estate left her child with a neighbour while she went to work.) This pattern

would seem to be typical of life in the Potteries. Mervyn Jones
in his social commentary said, 'I have pointed out that the
standard of living (in the Potteries) depends on two wage-
packets coming into the home, normally those of man and wife.
Nowadays a mother is back (at work) within at most six months
from the birth of a child, assuming she can find someone to look
after it.[1] The fact that out of the 34 respondents at Aston, only
eight did not go out to work, helped to explain the difficulty
experienced by these eight in finding people to talk to on the
estate in the day-time. At the first interview, one young mother
who had moved from Birmingham told of her loneliness on the
estate, particularly as her husband's work kept him away from
home for much of the week. However, she expressed her intention of starting a coffee-morning group to rectify this situation.
By the second interview, she had tried in vain to find others who
would participate in this type of activity. 'There is just no-one
around in the day-time', she explained, 'they are all out at
work.'

All but two of the 34 Aston families had lived within a radius
of 10 miles of the estate before moving to their new homes
(26 within a five-mile radius). The majority of them regarded
the Potteries as their area of origin.

HUNTLEY

The Huntley estate was found to be heterogeneous with respect
to both age and social class. One factor that almost certainly
influenced this, was the size and the price of the bungalows that
constituted most of the estate. Having two bedrooms, they were
suited only to small households. In consequence their residents
tended to be either single, or retired, or at the beginning of their
married lives. (Two of the bungalows were occupied by single
professional people.) There were few children on the estate.
Only two families had more than one child and they each lived
in one of the houses.

Half of the estate population already knew the Huntley area,
either because they had been brought up in the district or
because they had lived there prior to their move. The attraction
of this particular estate for most of the respondents, was the fact

[1] M. Jones, *Potbank*, Secker, 1961, pp. 175–6.

that it was 'in the country'. For a few of them, like the couple who had retired from West Bromwich, rural living was a new experience.

GARTON

The Garton estate consisted principally of young couples who had moved into their bungalows soon after marriage. (Three couples had lived with either the husband's or the wife's parents while they saved for their home or awaited its completion.) At the first interview, all but three of the 15 house-wives seen on Hill Close, were working full-time. However, by the second interview, this figure had been considerably reduced in response to the arrival, or impending arrival, of babies. All but two of the husbands held skilled or semi-skilled jobs, typically as a welder or fitter. The two exceptions were a sales representative and an electrical engineer. Although the latter was buying a home for the first time after living in a flat for several years, he clearly had aspirations for a bigger house and a better job, so his wife only anticipated living on the estate for a short time.

All of the Garton respondents had lived near the Potteries previously and all but two of them originated in the area.

GRASMERE, WIXLEY

On the Grasmere estate there were families at all stages, from the couples with a very young and expanding family, through those with children of secondary-school age, to the two widows who had bought their new homes for their retirement. For these widows, the question on geographical and job mobility was inapplicable, but of the remaining respondents, 80% said that an employment change in the future would certainly lead to a move. However, as Table 14 indicates, only three of the 12 respondents gave a change of job as the reason for their recent move. The desire for a larger house had been a more common inducement to move. Table 13, showing the distance of the move, underestimates the real distance of movement for the Grasmere Close population. The explanation for this lies in the fact that, because the development period of the houses was so long, three families had been forced to take temporary accommodation in the Wixley area while awaiting completion. If these three temporary moves had been omitted from the 0–10-mile category, one family would have been placed in the 11–50-mile category and two in the 51–100-mile category.

As one might expect with high-priced houses, there were husbands on this estate whose occupations fixed them in social class 1 on the Hall-Jones scale. However, classes 2 and 3 were also represented. (The widows were classified according to their late husband's occupation.) Clearly, some of the housewives had had a considerable amount of experience in adapting to a new residential environment. Table 12 shows that two of the respondents were living in the eighth home of their married lives, while one was in her tenth.

SKILBECK

The nine houses on the Skilbeck estate were occupied by respondents of varying ages. The three houses in the central section of the row each contained children of school age. All but one of the other households were childless. The exception was something of a special case for two reasons. First, the baby here was the only child below school age on the estate. Also, the husband was a manual worker on an estate of middle-class residents. This situation was perceived to offer an interesting test of social acceptance. The orientation of most of the members of this estate was towards North Staffordshire. Only one couple had close relations living elsewhere; for the most part parents lived within a 10-mile radius. One respondent had her elderly mother living with her, while another still had her grown-up daughters living at home. Nevertheless, three out of the nine respondents had spent part of their married lives in other regions of the country and had therefore had some experience of social integration into areas in which they were complete strangers.

UTTING

The small estate at Utting was found to be predominantly working class but with a wide age-range amongst its residents. The one respondent who regarded herself as something of a foreigner to the district, had lived less than 10 miles away before her marriage and subsequent occupation of the bungalow. While contented for the present, she expressed hopes of returning to her area of origin eventually. For the other estate members, all their family ties were within the Utting area or its immediate environs.

CHURCH CLOSE, WIXLEY

Church Close contained a heterogeneous population with respect to social class, but the respondents fell fairly neatly into two age groups. The 'young' group consisted of five housewives, four of whom went out to work. Of these four, two had a child under school age who was cared for in the daytime by relations living nearby. The 'old' group was composed of two old-age pensioners, one widowed, and a housewife estimated to be in her 50s.

General characteristics of the study population

The study population as a whole consisted predominantly, though not exclusively, of housewives between the ages of 20 and 40 (74 % of the total falling within this group). 47 % of the ladies had children of primary-school age or below, but this did not necessarily prevent them from working. Only 55 % of the respondents were at home all day; of the wives who went out to work, by far the highest proportion, 79 %, had a full-time job.

The social-class distribution of the respondents is interesting. None of the husbands were unskilled manual workers, i.e. in the Hall-Jones class 7. Perhaps one might have expected this since class 7 occupations would probably offer inadequate security for a home-loan. Nevertheless, 15 % of the respondents fell in class 6, the semi-skilled manual group, and 25 % in class 5, the skilled manual group. However, only six out of the 158 respondents (4 %) had husbands in class 4 which consists of the lower-grade inspectional and supervisory workers such as costing clerks or shop supervisors. This tends to confirm Goldthorpe and Lockwood's conclusion that the more affluent members of the working class are surpassing sections of the middle class in ownership of durable goods, in this case, of their own homes.[1]

There was a wide range of geographical mobility experience (as measured by the number of homes) in the whole study population, but for the most part the respondents were living in

[1] *op. cit.*, pp. 18–9.

their first, second or third home. While very few of the housewives already had plans for leaving the estate, a considerable proportion (46%), believed that a change in her husband's employment would precipitate a move; a further 15% admitted the possibility of a move under such circumstances. It would seem therefore, that Table 13, in showing that 69% of the respondents had made local moves, underestimated the mobile character of the study population. (This high figure for local moves may be partly explained by the fact that 20% of the housewives moved into their new homes because they had only recently been married; not perhaps, the best moment in time for the future husband to change his job.) While the aim of the study had been to focus on mobile families and their socialization into a strange area, the variation in the study population with respect to both mobility history and future expectation of movement, did permit an assessment of the differential effect of these factors on estate activity levels.

The inevitable question arises as to whether the study population is truly representative of purchasers of new houses. The statistics that are available for Great Britain, all refer to the mortgage-raising section of the community. It is likely, therefore, that older people are under-represented in these tables, since they are more likely to pay cash for their new houses, particularly if they are selling a larger house to purchase a smaller one for their retirement. A direct comparison between the official statistics on the age of borrowers and the data from this study, is hampered by the different classifications. However, the age structure of the study population appears to approximate to the national one. For example, in 1966 in the United Kingdom, 67% of purchasers of new dwellings, were aged between 21 and 34,[1] while the study population contained 74% under the age of 40. The distribution of borrowers according to occupation is more difficult to discover. However, a survey of house purchasers, conducted by the Cooperative Permanent Building Society, shows that during the period December 1967–March 1968, 41·6% of the people who borrowed money from them to purchase new dwellings were wage-earners, while

[1] *Housing Statistics: Great Britain*, no. 9, Apr. 1968, H.M.S.O., Table 44, p. 52, 'Building Societies: No. Mortgages by Age of Borrower'.

52·2% were salaried workers.[1] (The remaining 6·2% were
either retired or in the Defence Services.) Their 'wage-earners'
correspond approximately to the members of the Hall-Jones
classes 5–7, i.e. the manual workers, while their 'salaried-
workers' correspond to classes 1–4. It will be recalled that in the
study population, some 40% fell into the first group, i.e.

TABLE 8   *The social class distribution in the study population of 158 respondents*

Estate	Social Class*							TOTAL
	1	2	3	4	5	6	7	—
Whitemarsh	2	32	13	—	—	—	—	47
Aston	—	—	4	3	16	11	—	34
Huntley	1	4	6	1	8	4	—	24
Garton	—	1	1	—	8	6	—	16
Grasmere	3	5	4	—	—	—	—	12
Skilbeck	1	5	2	—	1	—	—	9
Utting	—	—	1	—	4	3	—	8
Church Close	—	2	1	2	3	—	—	8
TOTAL	7	49	32	6	40	24	—	158

* Derived by locating the occupation of the chief earner of the family
(usually the respondent's husband) on the Hall-Jones Scale.

TABLE 9   *The age distribution in the study population of 158 respondents*

Estate	Age of respondent (estimated)					TOTAL
	20–29	30–39	40–49	50–59	60 and over	
Whitmarsh	24	11	7	2	3	47
Aston	24	4	3	3	—	34
Huntley	10	4	1	4	5	24
Garton	11	5	—	—	—	16
Grasmere	5	2	3	1	1	12
Skilbeck	4	2	2	—	1	9
Utting	2	4	—	1	1	8
Church Close	4	1	—	1	2	8
TOTAL	84	33	16	12	13	158

[1] Cooperative Permanent Building Society, 'Who Buys Houses? (1968)', *Occasional Bulletin*, no. 87, Oct. 1968.

equivalent to the 'wage-earners', while the remianing 60 % fell into the second group, equivalent to the 'salaried-workers.' Allowing for the fact that in the study population the retired persons were classified according to their former occupations, and hence did not form a separate category, the Building Society and the research percentages are very similar. Thus, it would appear that on the basis of both age and occupation, the study population does not differ significantly from the general body of purchasers of new dwellings from which it was drawn.

TABLE 10   *The work situation of 158 respondents by the age of their children*

| Estate | Work situation when the respondent has | | | | | | | |
| | Children under 12 | | | | No children under 12 | | | |
	Full-time	Part-time	None	Total	Full-time	Part-time	None	Total
Whitmarsh	—	2	24	26	10	—	11	21
Aston	6	4	8	18	15	1	—	16
Huntley	1	2	3	6	8	1	9	18
Garton	1	—	4	5	6	—	5	11
Grasmere	1	—	9	10	—	1	1	2
Skilbeck	—	—	4	4	3	—	2	5
Utting	—	1	2	3	2	1	2	5
Church Close	1	1	1	3	2	1	2	5
TOTAL	10	10	55	75	46	5	32	83

TABLE 11   *The expected future geographical mobility of 158 respondents*

| Estate | With a change in the husband's job | | | | TOTAL |
	Likely to move	Might move	Unlikely to move	Not applicable*	
Whitmarsh	29	7	6	5	47
Aston	12	7	15	—	34
Huntley	11	—	7	6	24
Garton	5	3	8	—	16
Grasmere	8	2	—	2	12
Skilbeck	5	2	1	1	9
Utting	—	3	4	1	8
Church Close	3	—	3	2	8
TOTAL	73	24	44	17	158

TABLE 11 *cont.*

Estate	Likely to move	During the next year Might move	Unlikely to move	TOTAL
Whitmarsh	1	9	37	47
Aston	1	3	30	34
Huntley	1	1	22	24
Garton	2	—	14	16
Grasmere	—	1	11	12
Skilbeck	2	1	6	9
Utting	1	—	7	8
Church Close	—	2	6	8
TOTAL	8	17	133	158

* These respondents had purchased their houses for their retirement.

TABLE 12 *The past mobility behaviour of the 158 respondents as measured by the number of homes in which they had lived during their married lives*

Estate	No. homes in married life 1	2	3	4	5	6	7	8	9	10	TOTAL
Whitmarsh	9	17	12	4	3	1	—	1	—	—	47
Aston	14	11	9	—	—	—	—	—	—	—	34
Huntley	6	13	2	1	—	1	1	—	—	—	24
Garton	11	3	2	—	—	—	—	—	—	—	16
Grasmere	—	6	1	1	—	1	—	2	—	1	12
Skilbeck	2	4	3	—	—	—	—	—	—	—	9
Utting	3	5	—	—	—	—	—	—	—	—	8
Church Close	1	4	2	1	—	—	—	—	—	—	8
TOTAL	46	63	31	7	3	3	1	3	—	1	158

TABLE 13 *The distance of the move to the new homes: 158 respondents*

Estate	Distance of the last move (miles) 0–10	11–50	51–100	101–200	200+	TOTAL
Whitmarsh	14	20	4	7	2	47
Aston	32	2	—	—	—	34
Huntley	16	7	1	—	—	24
Garton	15	1	—	—	—	16
Grasmere	10	2	—	—	—	12
Skilbeck	7	2	—	—	—	9
Utting	8	—	—	—	—	8
Church Close	7	—	—	1	—	8
TOTAL	109	34	5	8	2	158

TABLE 14 *The principal reason given for the last move: 158 respondents*

Estate	Reason for the last move							TOTAL
	Husband's job	Recently married	To own	For a larger house	For better house/area	For retirement	Other	
Whitmarsh	23	8	4	4	4	4	—	47
Aston	2	12	10	2	4	—	4	34
Huntley	3	3	5	—	4	6	3	24
Garton	—	6	5	—	3	—	2	16
Grasmere	3	—	1	5	1	2	—	12
Skilbeck	2	1	1	3	2	—	—	9
Utting	—	2	2	—	2	1	1	8
Church Close	—	—	2	—	—	1	5	8
TOTAL	33	32	30	14	20	14	15	158

3 The Early Social Life on the Estates

'Moving in'

The statistical analysis which forms the core of this study is principally concerned with the social life of the estates as recorded at the second series of interviews. It will be recalled that these interviews were conducted approximately one year after the completion of the estates. It is fitting that a short account of the social life of the early months should precede the description of the analytical results.

In response to his investigations on local-authority housing estates, Mogey claimed that the first six months of estate life constitute a single phase. This phase was characterised by 'friendliness . . . and the continuous sharing of equipment and news.'[1] However, on the private estates it was discovered that this early period consisted of not one, but three stages.

The first stage occupied the one or two months when the first families were moving into their homes. Preparing and moving into one of the newly-completed houses at that stage demanded something of a pioneering spirit. Roads were unmade, hot water for scrubbing was difficult to obtain and conditions generally were such that each household was preoccupied with its own problems. In this situation, there appeared to be no recognition of the fact that other families were repeating the battle elsewhere on the estate. There was no evidence of Mogey's 'friendliness' or 'sharing of equipment'. Any help that

[1] Morris and Mogey, *op. cit.*, p. 42.

was received at this time, came from friends living elsewhere. Contact between these pioneers was virtually non-existent. It was only after they had settled down that philanthropic activity developed on the estates.

The arrival of the majority of the families marked the second stage. By this time, the existing residents held a superior position in that they commanded the facilities of electricity, water and gas. Whether or not they offered the use of these facilities to the newcomers seems to have been an arbitrary affair. It is difficult, even on specific estates, to decide why one person qualified for assistance rather than another. However, it is true to say that few of the earliest residents deliberately set out to help all newcomers, regardless of their location. Rather, when help was offered, it tended to be to the people who were moving in either next door or opposite. The arbitrariness of assistance generally, may have been reinforced by seasonal factors. This was certainly the case at Aston. Here the winter weather apparently deterred potential helpers. Although 13 houses were completed and occupied between November 1965 and March 1966, only three of their householders were offered help, and then from existing aquaintances in the road rather than from strangers.

The third stage consisted of the period in which the last few families arrived. It was common for these latecomers to receive no help whatsoever, even when they were surrounded by established residents. For example, a woman on the Whitmarsh estate had as a next-door neighbour, a person who in the early days of the estate had been the general source of assistance to several newcomers. Nevertheless, she had made no attempt to help this late arrival. Such a situation may be explained if one explores the motivation for helping newcomers. From the many relevant comments heard on the estates, two motives strongly suggest themselves. These are sympathy and gregariousness. It is probably impossible to identify which of these incentives was the more powerful on any specific occasion. While the individual's experience of moving was uppermost in her memory, it is feasible that her sympathy for fellow-sufferers would be at an optimum. After the lapse of several months when such memories would have been fading, it seems that helpful activity diminished likewise. If the incentive to help a new neighbour had been the desire, in so doing, to make a friend, after several months of this behaviour, such a desire may well have been satiated. Certainly the originally helpful person cited above, had made a multiplicity of friends by the time her new neighbour moved in. It was not only at Whitmarsh that complaints of neglect were voiced by latecomers. One respondent at Aston, for example, said with feeling,' I should have greatly appreciated assistance and companionship in the early days, but none was forthcoming.'

Early visiting

It has already been stated that social contact was virtually non-existent in the earliest months of estate life. Visiting tended to develop as the estate was filling up. During the first series of interviews, information was not only obtained on the identity of the early visitors, but also on the circumstances under which the initial invitations to visit were extended. Table 15 summarises the replies.

One of the most striking features of Table 15 is that each estate differed over the most commonly employed means of making social contact. For instance, on the Whitmarsh estate invitations were extended most often during casual conversations in the road or across the gardens. At Aston, on the other hand, social overtures were made most frequently when neighbours were offering to help each other after their moves. Somewhat surprisingly for new estates, it was only in one case that mutual complaints about the houses were responsible for drawing residents together. The shoddy workmanship in the bungalows on that estate, prompted one respondent after another to invite her neighbour in to view the poor plaster-work. This inspection was invariably accompanied by some form of hospitality.

The problems associated with young children, certainly drew mothers together. For example, at Whitmarsh several respondents called on one housewife to enquire about the local doctor or clinic, and found her to be a very friendly, helpful person who utilised the opportunity offered by these calls, to invite them in for coffee. She later held a jewellery-party to introduce these estate people to each other. In a sense she served as the social

TABLE 15   *The mechanics of early visiting*

Means by which the initial invitations were extended	Estate								TOTAL
	Whit.	Ast.	Hunt.	Gart.	Gras.	Skil.	Ut.	Ch. Cl.	
Help with the move	5	3	6	1	—	11	—	1	27
Help after the move	5	17	3	2	2	—	—	—	29
Chatted in road/ garden during the move	9	—	—	5	1	1	1	—	17
Chatted in road/ garden after the move	11	9	3	2	2	2	5	1	35
Known before	1	5	13	6	3	—	2	2	32
Related	—	3	1	—	—	—	2	—	6
Through the children	2	2	—	—	5	—	—	—	9
Through the husbands	—	7	2	—	—	—	2	—	11
Through another estate member	2	4	—	1	—	1	—	—	8
Deliberate call to extend invitation	1	4	—	—	8	2	—	—	15
Tupperware party	—	14	—	—	—	—	—	—	14
Other	1	6	5	—	1	—	—	—	13
Don't know	—	1	3	—	1	—	—	—	5
TOTAL	37	75	36	17	23	17	12	4	221

focus of the estate, occupying a central geographical position and socially fulfilling a significant role in linking members of Dorchester Close and Uppingham Close. At Aston, the respondents who lived at the 'closed' end of the cul-de-sac, explained that their intervisiting had started when the child at 36 and the one at 31 had each been ill soon after occupation. In these cases the people living nearby had helped with washing or shopping, and visiting developed as a result.

The husbands were responsible for the first social contacts between the young, childless wives in the central section of Jersey Close. When the husbands started meeting each other frequently at the local pub, they suggested that while they were there, the wives might like to congregate at one of their homes for coffee. This prompted one wife to give a Tupperware party to introduce the women to each other. This was followed in the next three or four months, by three more Tupperware parties, always attended by the same nucleus of seven women, but sometimes drawing in others from either end of the Close. Thereafter, the central group of couples started going out together for a Saturday-night drink or an evening at the local night-club, adjourning to one of the homes for coffee afterwards. (These Saturday-night excursions were still operating when the respondents were interviewed in 1967.)

Three general points arise concerning the nature of the early visiting on the estates. These refer to the frequency of visiting, the location of visiting pairs and the time of day in which the visiting occurred.

During their first three months on the estate, respondents seldom reported involvement in regular visiting. Few individuals had visited each other more than once in that time. The reciprocation of invitations was often postponed by housewives who believed that their homes were not yet fit for entertaining. This situation was particularly common on the estates where a number of families had moved a considerable distance and had therefore been unable to do much preparatory work on their houses prior to occupation.

Since many of the visits were initiated through casual contacts, they tended to involve people who lived close to each other. The exceptions to this appeared to fall into two categories.

If one family had lived in isolation for any length of time with only partially completed houses in the vicinity, the housewife often bridged the physical gap between herself and her nearest neighbours in order to establish some social contacts. Such was the case for example, between two respondents on the Grasmere development: these were physically as far apart as they could possibly have been. Nevertheless, they did visit each other while they were the sole occupants of the estate. The second category involved the intervention of some external agent. For instance, at Whitmarsh, the people who lived in the flats at the far end of Meadowside, and who themselves did not belong to the estate, made a point of welcoming the newcomers to the estate. A number of early arrivals were invited to the flats for coffee and it was by this means that the respondents at 3 Uppingham Close and 7 Dorchester Close first met socially. Thereafter, they visited each other independently of the flat-dwellers. Or again at Whitmarsh, the respondents at 8 Dorchester Close and 8 Meadowside first met, and started visiting each other, when the coalman delivered the former's coal to the latter, in error.

There was a relationship between the period in which the visiting occurred and the household members involved. The inclusion or exclusion of the husband depended on the wife's work situation. If she had no job, visiting took place in the daytime and in consequence, her husband was rarely involved. On the other hand, for the wife who worked, entertaining was naturally in the evenings or at the weekends, and usually included the husband.

The development of estate social life

Because the housewives were interviewed on the two separate occasions, it was possible to compare certain features of the early social life with the situation a year later. These features refer to both the number and the location of the persons who had been visited on each occasion, and to the attitude of the respondents towards the other people on the estate. These three aspects will be considered in turn.

It can be seen from Table 16, that the mean number of persons visited rose between the Stage I and Stage II interviews on

E

five out of the eight estates. It should be noticed however, that, with the exception of Huntley, it was the small estates that showed an apparent contraction in the range of acquaintances between the two dates. It is possible that, because of the small size of these estates, the residents had been able to complete their exploratory visiting before the Stage II interviews and had already 'selected' the individuals with whom they wished to interact on a regular basis. The number of estate members who had at some stage been visited by any particular individual, was naturally greater than the means suggest. 47·64 % of the persons visited in the early days, had apparently been 'dropped' after one year; of the persons who were visited at Stage II, as many as 57·79 % were new contacts who had not been mentioned in the Stage I interviews. Furthermore, in the intervening period, probably other persons were visited, assessed and 'dropped'.

When a comparison is made of the mean functional-distance between visiting individuals at Stage I and Stage II, the smallest

TABLE 16 *The mean number of persons visited, and the mean functional-distance[1] between visitor and visited, shortly after occupation (I) and one year later (II)*

Estate	Mean no. persons visited		Mean functional-distance		Total no. respondents	
	I	II	I	II	I	II
Whitmarsh	1·39	2·96	3·77	4·17	28	47
Aston	1·97	2·41	2·60	2·63	33	34
Huntley	1·55	1·33	1·88	2·78	22	24
Garton	1·21	1·69	1·71	1·89	14	16
Grasmere	1·92	3·67	1·96	2·32	12	12
Skilbeck	1·67	0·56	1·73	1·40	9	9
Utting	1·88	1·88	1·73	1·67	8	8
Church Close	0·50	0·63	2·25	2·00	8	8
ALL ESTATES	1·58	2·21	2·43	3·09	134	158

[1] See note, p. 87.

estates prove to be atypical. From Table 16 it can be seen that on the five largest estates, respondents were travelling further afield for their visiting one year after arrival. This again tends to suggest that some selection process was operating during the first year of estate life. This question of selection, or the choice of 'suitable' friends, will be examined more systematically later in chapter 4.

It was unfortunate that the Stage I question on the friendliness of the other estate people, was not repeated at Stage II. However, when at the second interview the respondents were asked what attitude they thought the other residents would adopt towards a new neighbour, many comments were forthcoming to indicate a shift in opinion compared with a year previously. The contrast between the two series of comments, lends some support to the maxim that 'familiarity breeds contempt'. During that first year, the gossip and the inveterate borrower had been discovered by two respondents at Aston, to their cost; and the inquisitive women had been identified by several respondents at Whitmarsh. It seems worthwhile considering these respondent impressions of the people around them, in a little more detail, for there can be no doubt that they indicate a measure of 'normlessness' of a kind hitherto attributed to new working-class communities,[1] but not examined in the context of new private estates.

The initial reaction of the housewives to their new neighbours was generally a very favourable one. The verdict of approximately 50% of the respondents was 'very friendly'. While some of the remainder were non-committal on the basis that they had not lived on the estate long enough to judge, there were only two respondents who suggested that the people around them were unfriendly. Where a distinction was drawn between some members of the estate and others, it was usually made on the basis of age. For example, two young respondents at Skilbeck, while suggesting that the young residents were very friendly, indicated that the older ones 'don't mix readily'. This failure they attributed respectively, to the lack of opportunity to develop social skills through poor education, and to the fact that they had never learnt to organise their housework effect-

[1] J. Klein, *op. cit.*, pp. 233–69.

ively leaving themselves insufficient time for social intercourse. Interestingly, some of the respondents who claimed unqualified friendliness, attributed this to the homogeneous nature of the families around them. In giving her reason for the general friendliness, one member of the Jersey Close Tupperware group said, 'Well, they're all young round here'. Another person on the Aston estate, this time at the 'open' end of the Close, explained the phenomenon by the fact that, 'We all have children round here'. Strictly speaking, this was not true, but obviously a sufficiently large proportion of the families in her immediate vicinity did have children, thereby leaving her with this impression. However, an elderly lady at Whitmarsh felt that her exclusion from the manifestations of friendly behaviour she saw going on around her, was due to the fact that, 'They all have young children'. She seemed to have overlooked the fact that there were three other elderly housewives living in the road.

After one year on the estate, there appeared to be a consensus on norms at Utting, Skilbeck and Grasmere, Wixley. Comments frequently expressed on all three of these estates, were of the form: 'People here are friendly without being intrusive'; or 'The people here wouldn't push themselves, but they would help in an emergency'. At Garton and Whitmarsh, however, there had clearly been a considerable amount of uncertainty over the proper form of social behaviour.

Most of the Garton respondents had moved from predominantly working class areas where, one imagines from their comments, they had seen 'neighbouring' in operation. (By 'neighbouring' they meant 'popping in and out of each other's houses uninvited'.) Realising the dangers and difficulties to which this practice gives rise, some housewives were making a deliberate effort to prevent it developing. However, they were trying so hard that their efforts were being interpreted as unfriendly behaviour. Although there seemed to have been a general rejection of these old norms, no clearly defined or generally accepted code of behaviour for the new estate appeared to have emerged.

At Whitmarsh there were suggestions that the early pattern of behaviour was undergoing revision; as one middle-aged respondent hinted, 'A lot of them [the younger housewives] were rather too friendly at first and this led to gossiping and in consequence, they fell out.' The sort of incident that one imagines prompted her remark was reported by a young mother on Uppingham Close. She had been both annoyed and hurt when she had helped a new neighbour a great deal during an illness soon after she had moved in, and her motivation for this kindness had been misconstrued by the recipient as nosiness. Thereafter, both ladies had ignored each other. Another young mother referred to the gossiping on the estate. 'I don't like it here', she said, 'there are some people who want to know all about you and don't ask to your face but enquire of others. This is not just about me; they feel they ought to know about everybody.' This seems indicative of the general uncertainty that might be expected on such an estate, where the residents come from all parts of the country and have no immediate reference-group in older residents. The same respondent, in reinforcing the idea that this behaviour is characteristic of new, rather than old estates, explained, 'I have never experienced this before, but previously we lived on older estates, so possibly this is typical of new ones.' There was evidence that after the first year of life on the Whitmarsh estate, a method of making social overtures that was acceptable to most people, was emerging. Fundamentally it was based on reserve and hesitancy, in the belief that by adopting such an approach, one could not then be branded as overinquisitive. As one respondent put it, 'We (the ladies) chat on the way to the shops and in the gardens, but the men are more bold; but then they don't worry about being thought nosy.' According to this precept, visiting was by invitation only. In spite of this and the earlier uncertainty over norms, a great deal of visiting was reported at Whitmarsh.

This introduces the whole question of the determinants of visiting levels. Therefore, the quantitative analysis which was designed to identify these determinants will now be discussed.

4 Quantitative Analysis

The results of this quantitative analysis will be considered under two main headings: the regression analysis and the sociometric analysis. The regression model will be examined for its contribution to the explanation of visiting levels on' the housing estates; the sociometric analysis will indicate the extent and the nature of social group formation on the estates. At the end of the chapter, it will be shown that a reconciliation of these two approaches is essential for a more complete and satisfactory explanation of friendship formation on these new housing estates.

The regression analysis

It will be recalled that the purpose of the regression analysis was threefold. First, in correlating the individual's activity (visiting) level (Y) with possible explanatory variables, it was hoped to identify the determinants of visiting levels and also to establish the magnitude of their influence. Second, on the basis of this correlation[1] analysis, suitable variables would be selected for incorporation in the regression model. This model would then be used to calculate several series of values: the expected, or predicted activity level for each individual (Y'), the difference between Y' and Y, and a mean value of $Y-Y'$ for each of the eight estates. Third, by the use of ranking methods it was hoped to show that planning and other estate characteristics explained

[1] See Statistical Glossary.

the estate ordering on $\overline{Y-Y'}$ (i.e. the mean estate value for the difference between expected and achieved activity).

THE CORRELATION ANALYSIS

Preparing the data for the correlation analysis proved to be the most tedious and time-consuming stage in the whole research process. The reason for this was as follows. In the general case, the correlation operation demands that at least one of the two variables to be correlated should be approximately normally distributed.[1, 2] However, in this case each pair of variables was to be correlated in turn, thereby producing a 24 x 24 matrix of simple correlation coefficients. In consequence, it was necessary for the distributions of all the 24 variables to approximate to normality. An examination of their frequency distributions showed that many of the variables, including Y itself, were highly skewed.[2] Thus, it was essential to transform[2] Y and these other variables to normality. It was then necessary to test each variable, including the transformed ones, against Y transformed. This last operation was to ensure that each bore a linear relationship to transformed Y. A description of the procedure employed in transforming Y to $\log_e (Y+1)$ is to be found in Appendix III. In the same appendix is a list of the other 23 variables with, where applicable, their transformations.

The matrix of simple correlation coefficients reproduced in Appendix IV, shows that seven of the 23 variables tested, correlated significantly with activity. These seven significant variables are listed in Table 17 with their appropriate correlation coefficients (see p. 61).

THE SIGNIFICANT VARIABLES

Private estates were deliberately chosen for this study in the expectation that their residents would have no existing family ties in the area. However, five pairs of relations were discovered on the estates themselves; two pairs at Aston and one pair each at Garton, Utting and Huntley. Because these 10 respondents

[1] G. W. Snedecor and W. G. Cochran, *Statistical Methods*, Iowa State University Press, 1967, p. 185.
[2] See Statistical Glossary.

already had a given relationship on the estate, it was important to make some provision for the possible inflationary effect of this on their visiting scores. Accordingly, a dummy variable[1, 2] was employed in the correlation analysis. This dummy variable indicated the possession or otherwise, of a relation on the estate. It was seen in Table 17 that this variable correlated highly significantly with estate activity showing that the presence of a relation was indeed associated with an increase in the number of estate visits.

The significant correlation between activity and age reveals that as the individual gets older, she is likely to make fewer visits to other estate members. This finding qualifies that of Willmott and Young. It will be recalled that they discovered an inverse relationship between age and the amount of all non-relation visiting.[3] It is now possible to say that the relationship they observed in the general situation also applies in the more specific situation of the estate.

The association between geographical mobility expectation and activity is of particular interest because the concept of mobility expectation appears to be a relatively novel one in British sociological research. When Fellin and Litwak related future mobility expectation to neighbourhood integration in the U.S., they found that the person who was most likely to integrate into the present neighbourhood group was the one who expected to move away with a change in her husband's job; or in their terms, who had 'a future reference to a different neighbourhood group.'[4] Their result is not directly comparable to this because they were measuring neighbourhood integration by the number of persons known in the neighbourhood, rather than by the activity level within it. Nevertheless, the two results tend to reinforce each other since in this study the people who made the most neighbourhood visits were likely to be those

---

[1] For the justification for the use of dummy variables in correlation and regression analyses, see J. Johnston, *Econometric Methods*, McGraw-Hill, 1963, pp. 221–8; also K. W. Smillie, *An Introduction to Regression and Correlation*, Academic Press, 1966, pp. 69–70.

[2] See Statistical Glossary.

[3] Willmott and Young, *op. cit.*, p. 107.

[4] Fellin and Litwak, *op. cit.*, p. 371.

TABLE 17 *The significant simple correlation coefficients between activity and other variables*

Variable number	Variable	Correlation coefficient	Significance level	Explanation
10	Relative on the estate	+0·3249	0·001	Activity rate increases when a relative lives on the estate
2	Age	+0·2424*	0·01	Activity rate decreases with age
8	Geographical mobility expectation	+0·2388	0·01	Activity rate increases as the certainty of a future move intensifies
11	Number of cars	+0·2163	0·01	Activity rate increases with the number of cars in the household
23	Number of children under 5	—0·2138*	0·01	Activity rate increases with the number of children under 5 years of age
14	Gave help to a newcomer	+0·1668	0·05	Activity rate is highest for the people who helped a newcomer to the estate
20	Proportion of the estate occupied on arrival	—0·1657	0·05	Activity rate is highest for the earliest arrivals on the estate

* A reciprocal transformation was employed on these variables. Thus the sign of the correlation coefficient appears to be contrary to expectation.

housewives for whom job mobility implied geographical mobility.

On the basis of earlier research findings, it was argued in Chapter I that any relationship between the number of family cars and activity on the estate, would be a negative one. It was thought that the extra family car where it existed, would enable the housewife to maintain relationships away from the estate[1] and thereby diminish her social activity on the estate. However, the correlation analysis has shown that estate activity correlated significantly, and positively, with the number of family cars. Indeed, there is no evidence of any association between the number of cars and the amount of visiting with friends, or relations living off the estate. Rather, the explanation for the correlation between the number of cars and activity on the estate, probably lies in the fact that the former is a function of mobility expectation which itself correlated with activity.[2]

The exploratory work on the role of children in determining estate activity levels (see Appendix III), showed that when the possession of children under the age of five was treated as a dummy variable[3] and correlated with activity, it bore a stronger association with it than either the possession of children under 12 or under 21, respectively. Clearly, activity tends to be highest when the housewife has young children. While the measures were not directly comparable, this appears to support the finding of Hodges and Smith that the dependence on the neighbourhood as a source of friends increases with the birth of children and declines thereafter.[4] However, the argument was carried one stage further in this study. It was thought that if the birth of the first child increased the mother's dependence on the neighbourhood and induced visiting activity in the immediate locality, the birth of each subsequent child would further intensify localised visiting. Therefore, estate activity was correlated with the actual number of children under the age of

[1] J. Klein, *op. cit.*, p. 332.
[2] When the partial correlation coefficients (see Statistical Glossary) were examined, it was found that the correlation between activity and the number of family cars fell from significance at the 1% level to significance at the 5% level when the effect of mobility expectation was held constant.
[3] We see no way to avoid this pun!
[4] *op. cit.*, p. 111.

five. This yielded a higher correlation coefficient than the equivalent dummy variable. It would appear, therefore, that the more young children a mother has, the more intense her visiting activity on the estate is likely to be. However, this estate visiting associated with the possession of young children, would in Hodges and Smith's terms be explained by the physical confinement of the mother to the estate. This being so, one would expect to find a negative correlation between the number of young children and the number of visits to friends off the estate. However, no significant association was found between these two variables. One must, therefore, conclude at this stage that with the arrival of children, estate friends do not necessarily become an alternative to friends elsewhere, but rather, that visiting with estate members develops because they happen to be conveniently situated during the period of child-rearing when the housewife has more time for visiting generally.

The last two variables to correlate significantly with activity each refer to some aspect of the housewife's early experience on the estate. These variables are the dummy one 'gave help to a newcomer' and the proportion of the estate that was occupied when the individual took up residence on it. (Obviously these variables are less than perfect. However outgoing a person might be she stands little chance of extending help to other newcomers if the estate is almost occupied when she herself arrives. At the same time the arrival of 'helpers' is likely to be random throughout the estates; the only source of systematic bias is the differential rate of occupation.) The significant association between activity and the behavioural variable 'gave help' indicates that it was the individuals who made a helpful gesture to at least one new neighbour, who tended to have the highest visiting rate after a year on the estate. The negative correlation between activity and the proportion of the estate occupied, suggests that it was the earliest arrivals who were the most active after a year of estate life. (Although this correlation is only significant at the 5 % level,[1] 'the proportion of the estate occupied' is validated as a measure, by its highly significant correlation with another independent variable, the number of months spent in the house.)

[1] See Statistical Glossary.

THE NON-SIGNIFICANT VARIABLES

Of the 16 independent variables that failed to correlate significantly with activity, there are several that require special comment. They are social class, the indices of past mobility, the amount of visiting to extra-estate friends and relations respectively, and the attitudinal measures.

It is interesting that while the expectation of future geographical mobility correlated significantly with activity, neither social class nor the indices of past mobility did so. Nevertheless, social class was validated as a measure by its correlation with mobility expectation itself and with each of the indices of past mobility, namely the number of homes previously occupied, the distance of the move and the distance from the respondent's area of origin.[1] This failure to find a significant relationship between activity and either social class or past mobility, sheds fresh light on earlier research.

The work of Elizabeth Bott will be considered first. As a criterion of the physical mobility of her families, she used 'the total number of areas lived in by each husband and wife.' Even while admitting that 'the numbers are too small to be taken very seriously', she still claimed that 'it is evident that on the average, the families with loose-knit networks had lived in far more places than those with medium-knit, transitional, and close-knit networks.'[2] One must accept that she was not asserting the obverse to be true, namely that all the families, mobile by her definition, were in loose-knit networks. However, when she described the relationship that her loose-knit families had towards their neighbourhood, it would appear that she was treating loose-network connectedness and physical mobility as synonymous. At the same time, she was introducing yet another criterion of mobility – the fact that couples were not living in the neighbourhood in which they were brought up – when she wrote, 'These husbands and wives (in loose-knit networks) did

---

[1] Earlier research provides evidence of this association between social class and indices of mobility. For example, Friedlander and Roshier, and Douglas and Blomfield have found a strong relationship between the distance of the move and social class. See Friedlander and Roshier, *op. cit.*, pp. 50–1; and J. W. B. Douglas and J. M. Blomfield, *Children under Five*, Allen & Unwin, 1958, p. 27. For further evidence see Willmott and Young, *op. cit.*, p. 30; Fellin and Litwak, *op. cit.*, p. 368; Musgrove, *op. cit.*, pp. 46–9.

[2] Bott, *op. cit.*, p. 106.

not regard the neighbourhood as a source of friends. In most cases the husband and wife had moved several times both before and after marriage, and none of them were living in the neighbourhood in which they had grown up. . . . In all cases these husbands and wives were polite but somewhat distant to most neighbours.'[1]

If Bott's findings are valid, one might expect two series of results to emerge in the present study. First, there should be a significant but negative correlation between activity and the number of homes in the respondent's married life, and also between activity and the number of miles of the respondent from her area of origin. (Each of these measures of past physical mobility being approximately equivalent to the ones that Bott used.) In fact neither of these correlation coefficients proved to be significant. Second, on the basis that the loose-knit and mobile families find their friends outside the neighbourhood, one would expect to find a positive association between the number of visits to friends off the estate and each of the two indices of mobility, namely, the number of previous homes and the distance from the respondent's area of origin. Neither of these two correlation coefficients was significant.

Now let us consider the work of Willmott and Young. They found a social-class gradient in visiting: the people in the lowest occupational grouping participating the least in non-relation visiting.[2] While they did not differentiate between visiting within the neighbourhood and elsewhere, if their conclusion is generally valid one would expect to observe a significant correlation between either social class and the amount of within-estate visiting, or social class and the amount of extra-estate visiting to friends, or both. However, neither correlation was significant. Recalling that there was a significant correlation in this study between social class and geographical mobility expectation and between geographical mobility expectation and activity, it might be that what Willmott and Young observed was not the effect of social class on visiting but rather, the effect of the geographical mobility expectation component of social class on visiting.

[1] *ibid.*, p. 75.
[2] *op. cit.*, p. 109.

Fellin and Litwak discovered that the presence of relations in the same residential area was detrimental to neighbourhood integration.[1] The study data for the location of the respondents' parents is shown in Table 18.

TABLE 18 *The proximity of the respondents' parents*

Estate	Location of respondents' parents (miles)					Deceased	D.K.	TOTAL
	0-10	11-50	51-100	101-200	Over 200			
Whitmarsh	4	16	4	8	5	9	1	47
Aston	27	1	1	—	—	5	—	34
Huntley	9	5	1	1	—	8	—	24
Garton	13	1	—	2	—	—	—	16
Grasmere	2	2	2	—	—	6	—	12
Skilbeck	6*	1	—	—	—	2	—	9
Utting	6†	—	—	—	—	2	—	8
Church Close	5	—	—	—	—	3	—	8
TOTAL	72	26	8	11	5	35	1	158

* One respondent here had her mother actually living with her.

† This includes the mother at no. 8 who lived next-door to her daughter at no. 7

It can be seen from Table 18 that a considerable proportion of the respondents had parents living within a 10-mile radius of the housing estate. This proportion was high in the case of the estates such as Aston and Garton which were composed of low-price dwellings and which were situated close to the Potteries. The Potteries are renowned for their close-knit family networks and for the homogeneous working-class nature of the area. While all the estates were either on, or beyond, the fringe of this area, its influence is probably indicated in one of the findings of this study. There was a significant correlation between the number of visits to relations in the preceding month and social class. This showed that the members of the lower social classes (the manual groups) were likely to visit relations more frequently than the higher social classes (the non-manual groups).

In spite of the close proximity of many parents and contrary to expectation, the number of visits to relations did not significantly correlate with estate activity. It would appear therefore,

[1] *op. cit.*, p 373.

that the presence of relations in the area did not pose a threat to the establishment of social activity on the estates.

Since this was essentially a sociological study, psychological characteristics which might have influenced the individual's visiting activity level were not fully explored. Only two psychological measures were tested against activity. These crude measures were the individual's attitude towards privacy and the attitude she felt she ought to take towards a newcomer to the estate. However, neither of these variables correlated significantly with activity.

The absence of an association between activity and the attitude to a newcomer, would appear to run contrary to the findings of Fellin and Litwak in their Detroit and Buffalo studies.[1] However, the explanation for this may lie in the British housewife's failure, unlike her American counterpart, to act upon her convictions. If the people who said that one should offer help to a newcomer had in fact given help, the correlation between the attitudinal measure and the dummy variable 'gave help' should have been high. It was close to zero. Because the behavioural measure 'gave help' did correlate significantly with activity, it could be that the act of helpfulness indicated an outgoingness that the attitudinal measure failed to detect. In order to clarify this situation, there would seem to be a strong case for including personality tests in any future study of this type.

SUMMARY OF THE CORRELATION ANALYSIS

The results of this analysis of simple correlation coefficients lend support to the hypotheses that the individual's level of within-estate visiting depends respectively upon her age, the number of young children she has, her geographical mobility expectation and the number of cars in her household. Furthermore, the results have indicated that there is an association between the individual's activity level and whether or not she has a relative living on the estate, the stage in the development of the estate at which she arrived on it and her early behaviour on the estate as measured by whether or not she gave help to a new neighbour.

[1] *op. cit.*, p. 373.

In the absence of a significant correlation between the relevant variables and activity, it seems justifiable *at this stage* to reject the hypotheses that the individual level of within-estate visiting depends upon social class, the respondent's work situation, her past geographical mobility behaviour, her avowed attitude towards a newcomer and her social activity off the estate whether this is represented by the number of visits to friends, or to relations, or by the number of social clubs to which she belongs.

THE REGRESSION MODEL

It will be recalled that the principal reason for performing the regression analysis was to explain the differences in activity that were found to exist between the estates.[1] A necessary preliminary to the regression operation therefore, was to show that significant differences in activity between the estates did indeed exist. This was achieved by performing an analysis of variance[2] on the transformed Y data (see Table 19). The analysis of variance shows that the variation in activity between the estates

TABLE 19   *The analysis of variance of Y transformed*

Source of variation	Sum of squares	Degrees of freedom	Mean square	F
Between estates	21·6716	7	3·0959	2·8278
Within estates	164·2180	150	1·0948	
TOTAL	185·8896*	157		

* The slight discrepancy between the value for the total sum of squares in Tables 19 and 20 is attributable to the different computational facilities which were used.

[1] See Statistical Glossary. In actual fact there was another prior reason for carrying out the regression. Most of the ambiguity in the findings of previous work is due to the fact that conclusions about causes of friendship, visiting intensity, etc., are based on simple association tests and sometimes not even on these. In modern sociology it is sensible to use multiple regression as an alternative to these simple tests since then we can be sure that the contribution of X_i to Y is due to X_i alone and not due to the intervention of X_j, X_k etc. The proof of this particular pudding is in the comparison between Tables 17 and 21. It will be seen that some reasonably well correlated variables do not stand up to the much more rigorous test of regression.

[2] See Statistical Glossary.

was significantly greater than the variation within the estates. The variance ratio of $2\cdot83^1$ was significant at the 5% level. (At $P=0\cdot05$ with 7 and 150 degrees of freedom, $F=2\cdot76$.)[1]

The discussion of the simple correlation between activity and the independent variables ignored the possible effect on these relationships of the inter-correlation of the independent variables. The effect of such intercorrelations was observable in the matrix of first-order partial correlation coefficients. For example, it can be seen from the matrix of simple correlation coefficients (see Appendix IV), that apart from its significant correlation with activity, age was also significantly correlated with nine other variables. When the partial correlation coefficients $r_{y2\cdot3}$ $r_{y2\cdot4}{}^1$ etc., were considered, it was found that the correlation between age and activity fell below the 1% significance level when the effect of mobility expectation was held constant, and only just remained significant at the 1% level when the number of children under five years was held constant. On the other hand, while $r_{y2\cdot0}=0\cdot2424$, $r_{y2\cdot9}=0\cdot2817$, $r_{y2\cdot21}=0\cdot3128$ and $r_{y2\cdot15}=0\cdot3162$, showing that the association between age and activity became stronger when the effect was held constant of the respondent's work situation, her previous number of homes and the ownership situation in her previous home, respectively. Clearly, other variables were impinging on the relationship between activity and age. Therefore, in deriving a regression model for prediction purposes, it was vital to find a method of selecting the suitable variables for inclusion in the model that would control the intercorrelation between the independent variables. The step-wise regression method programmed by Smillie satisfied this condition.

This step-wise method operates in the following way. From the independent variables $X_1, X_2, X_3, ----- X_n$ it selects the variable, say X_4, which 'accounts for the largest proportion of the variation of the dependent variable'[2] and this is introduced first into the regression function.[3] On the basis of the first-order

---

[1] See Statistical Glossary.

[2] K. W. Smillie, *op. cit.*, p. 61.

[3] This variable is the one which correlates most strongly with the dependent variable, since the squares of the simple correlation coefficients r_{y2}, r_{y3} etc., show the proportion of the variation of the dependent variable Y, that is due to each of the interdependent variables.

F

partial correlation coefficients, a second variable is introduced into the regression function. This is the variable which 'accounts for the largest proportion of the remaining variation'.[1] Thereafter, each of the other independent variables are introduced into the regression in a similar manner. From the resulting series of n regression analyses it is possible to select the one which satisfies each of two conditions. First, the regression itself must be significant; second, the regression sum of squares must be a maximum while all the regression coefficients remain significant.

Using the Smillie-type programme on the study data, it was found that the regression analysis which fulfilled the two conditions stated above, contained five independent variables.[2] Together these five variables explained $27 \cdot 8\%$ of the variation in the dependent variable, activity. The analysis of variance for the regression (see Table 20) shows that the regression itself was significant at the $0 \cdot 5\%$ level. (At $P = 0 \cdot 005$ with 5 and 152 degrees of freedom, F is approximately equal to 3.55.)

TABLE 20 *The analysis of variance of the multiple regression*

Source of variation	Sum of squares	Degree of freedom	Mean square	F
Regreesion	51·6746	5	10·3349	11·71
Residuals	134·2076	152	0·8829	
TOTAL	185·8822	157		

The five independent variables which were included in the regression are listed in Table 21. Also shown is the contribution made by the first variable, and the additional contribution made by each of the other four variables, to the prediction of the dependent variable, as well as the t-values for the corresponding regression coefficients.

The regression equation derived from this analysis was as follows:

$$Y' = 0 \cdot 8068 + 1 \cdot 5840 \, X_{10} = 0 \cdot 2764 \, X_8 - 0 \cdot 4572 \, X_9 + 0 \cdot 6655 \, X_2 + 0 \cdot 3891 \, X_{14}$$

Thus the individual who could be expected to make the

[1] Smillie, *op. cit.*, p. 62.

[2] The significance of the regression coefficients was assessed from their t-values (see Statistical Glossary). The 5% significance-level was adopted as the critical one.

TABLE 21   *The Independent Variables in the Multiple Regression*

Variable number	Variable	% Contribution to the prediction	t-value	Signifi-cance level
10	Relative on the estate	10·56	5·06	0·001
8	Geographical mobility expecta-tion	7·02	3·24	0·005
9	Respondent's work situation	4·14	2·91	0·005
2	Age	3·16	2·70	0·01
14	Gave help	2·92	2·48	0·025
	TOTAL	27·80		

greatest number of visits on the estate, would have a relative living on the estate, would expect to move house if her husband changed his job, would be a full-time housewife, would be aged 20–29 and would have given help to a newcomer during the early days on the estate. When this equation was applied to the data for each of the 158 members of the study population, not many of them had a relative on the estate. Therefore, it could be said that in general the 'activists' on the estates were expected to be the young housewives who were at home all day and who, while not knowing how long they would be living on the estate, nevertheless were prepared to initiate social relationships there.

It is interesting to compare Table 21 showing the variables which appeared in the regression, with Table 17 listing the variables which individually correlated with activity. As one would expect from the regression selection procedure, the dummy variable indicating the presence of a relative on the estate reappeared in the regression. However, when its effect had been eliminated, it was mobility expectation which emerged as the next most powerful predictor of activity levels. On the basis of simple correlation coefficients alone, one might have expected age to be the second strongest predictor. In the step-wise regression, mobility expectation was succeeded by the respondent's work situation which had not quite reached signi-ficance when correlated originally with activity. However, when the first-order partial correlation coefficients were considered, it was noticeable that the correlation between activity and work situation became significant when the effect of mobility expectation and relatives were each held constant. The failure of the children variable to appear in the regression is probably attributable to the fact that the correlation between this variable and activity fell from being significant at the 1 % level to significance at the 5 % level on each occasion when age, mobility expectation and work situation were held constant.

Thus a considerable amount of reordering of the variables occurred between the correlation and regression analyses. This fact tends to indicate the danger of selecting variables for inclusion in a regression model purely on the basis of their simple correlations with the dependent variable.

The validity of this particular step-wise method, was established by performing the regression calculation on the same data, but this time using a step-down, rather than a step-up method. Briefly, the step-down method starts with the regression of all the independent variables on the dependent one and using a preordained criterion, eliminates the independent variables one at a time. It will be appreciated that this is the reverse procedure from the step-up method. As a warning for anyone comparing the results from the two methods, Snedecor and Cochran have reported that 'the step-up and step-down methods will not necessarily select the same X variables'. Where differences in the subsets of the X variables occur between the two methods, they suggested, 'the differences are not necessarily alarming, because when intercorrelations are high, different subsets can give almost equally good predictions.'[1]

When the regression was computed by the step-down method, the prediction was extremely close to the step-up one: 27·65 % compared with 27·80 %. This prediction was based on six, rather than five variables, but the four most powerful predictive variables were the same in either case. This agreement was most reassuring.

THE RANKING PROCEDURE

The regression analysis provided the facility for calculating each

[1] Snedecor and Cochran, *op. cit.*, p. 413.

individual's expected activity level. However, it will be recalled that the concern of this research was to explain activity-deviance or the deviation of actual, from expected, activity levels. It was suggested earlier that significant aspects of the physical environment would explain this activity-deviance. The identification of such aspects would be accomplished by deriving from the individual values, an estate value for activity-deviance; then the ranking of the eight estates on activity-deviance could be compared with their ranking on each planning feature. If the planning feature exerted a significant influence on activity-deviance, the two rankings of the estates would be very similar. This ranking procedure will be examined in this section.

A predicted, or expected activity level, Y', was calculated for each respondent by substituting the relevant values in the regression equation. (Thus Y' represents the number of visits that the individual would be expected to make if her activity was determined solely on the basis of the individual characteristics that were embodied in the regression model.) Then the regression residuals, $Y-Y'$, were derived. These represent the deviation of expected from actual activity. The frequency distribution of the regression residuals[1] is shown in figure 1. It can be seen from this that, as expected, the residuals are normally distributed.

To obtain the values for estate activity-deviance, the mean value of $Y-Y'$ was calculated for each of the estate populations. The ranking analysis was to be based on the assumption that the eight estates differed significantly on activity-deviance. An analysis of variance was employed to test for this. However, this analysis of variance on $Y-Y'$, in yielding a variance ratio of 1·26, failed to reach significance at the 5 % level.[2] The details of the analysis of variance appear in Appendix v. It was rather disturbing to find that the variation between estates on activity-deviance was not significantly greater than the variation within estates. Nevertheless, there was ample justification for continuing with the original ranking scheme. Such justification was to be found in a closer analysis of the estate means on $Y-Y'$.

[1] That is, the proportion of visiting frequency not explained by the explanatory variables.

[2] At P=0·05 with 7 and 150 degrees of freedom, F=2·07.

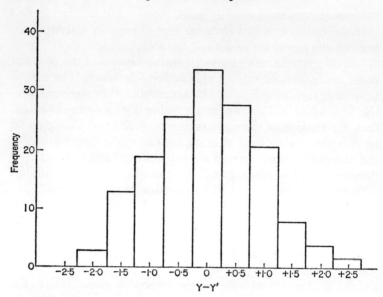

FIG. 1 Frequency distribution of the regression residuals for 158 respondents

FIG. 1 Frequency distribution of the regression residuals for 158 respondents

It can be seen from Table 22 that the estate means on $Y-Y'$ varied over a considerable range. The difference between every pair of estate means was tested for significance. An account of this procedure can be found in Appendix v. No significant difference was discovered between the means of any two estates of adjacent rank; therefore, statistical grouping was not possible. However, significant differences did exist between the means of estates which were high and those which were low on the ranking of $\overline{Y-Y'}$. Clearly these differences, and indeed the whole ordering on estate activity-deviance, required explanation. To this end, the ranking technique detailed initially was employed.

It was argued earlier that if the ordering of the estates on mean activity-deviance could be explained by one or more estate planning characteristics, the ranking of the estates on $\overline{Y-Y'}$ should be highly correlated with their ranking on the influential planning variable. In the ranking analysis, six

TABLE 22   *The estate values for the mean and Variance of Y- Y'*

Estate	Mean	Estate ranking on Mean	Variance
Utting	+0·7943	I	0·4190
Grasmere	+0·3029	2	0·5349
Whitmarsh	+0·1090	3	0·7917
Aston	+0·0422	4	0·9044
Huntley	+0·0369	5	0·8662
Garton	—0·2754	6	0·3719
Church Close	—0·6708	7	0·7425
Skilbeck	—0·8518	8	1·2858

planning variables were correlated with $Y-Y'$. These were:—
the site-plan, the size of the estate, two indices of the spacing of
the estate, and the mean and the standard deviation of the pur-
chase-price of the dwellings on the estate.

Since the relationship between the site-plan and estate
activity-deviance formed the core of this study, this will be considered first. It was suggested in Chapter 1 that the nucleated
estates would appear highest in the ranking of $\overline{Y-Y'}$, followed
by the cul-de-sacs, with the linear developments lowest in the
ranking. However, this did not prove to be the case. While one
of the linear developments, Skilbeck, did appear last in the rank
order, the other one, Utting, was first. It was only when the
means for similarly-planned estates were amalgamated, that the
expected ranking emerged, i.e. the group of nucleated estates
was found to have the highest ranking, descending to the linear
estates. However, no statistical justification can be advanced for
this procedure because the means of the grouped estates were
significantly different from each other. Thus, on the basis of the
ranking operation, the hypothesis that there is an association
between the site-plan and activity levels, must be rejected.

The size of the estate was measured by the number of
dwellings on it. The ranking on estate size was found to be very
poorly correlated with the ranking on $\overline{Y-Y'}$. (The complete
list of Spearman's rank correlation coefficients can be seen in
Appendix v.) Thus the number of dwellings on an estate would
not appear to influence its activity-deviance. Similarly, the
spacing or density of the estate, as measured by either the mean

hailing-distance or the mean physical-functional-distance between dwellings, would seem to be irrelevant too.[1]

The last two planning variables were both concerned with the purchase price of the estate dwellings. The mean purchase price was used as an indication of the general price-level on the estate, while the other, the standard deviation of purchase price, served as a measure of the degree of admixture of house-type. As with all the other planning variables, the correlation between the ranking on these and on mean activity-deviance was low.

Therefore, it would appear that the explanation for estate activity-deviance levels in the heterogeneous situations observed in this study, cannot be found in the planning characteristics of the estates. In seeking the explanation elsewhere, the rankings of other variables were tested for their association with the estate ranking on activity-deviance. These variables can be divided into three groups.

The first group contains the estate means on the variables which either were included in the significant regression or could meaningfully be related to estate activity-deviance, such as the attitudinal measures or the period since occupation. The second group consists of the standard deviations, rather than the means, of the variables included in the first group. Effectively, these were measures of the heterogeneity of each estate population on specific characteristics. The third group contains three socio-metric indices, a mutual pairs, a side-neighbour and a three-person clique index.[2] As stated earlier, the list of the Spearman rank correlation coefficients is to be found in Appendix v, but some results require special comment. For this purpose, each group of variables will be considered in turn.

As might be expected, the ranking of the estate means on each of the five regression variables, age, mobility expectation etc.,

---

[1] The 'hailing-distance' between estate dwellings was defined as the length of the imaginary line joining the two nearest doors of adjacent dwellings. The 'physical-functional-distance' was defined as the distance that a person would need to walk from her dwelling to the adjacent one using the quickest conventional route.

[2] These indices represent the ratio of the actual to the possible number of socio-metric relationships of a defined type on each particular estate. For example, the side-neighbour index is the ratio of the actual number of side-neighbour relation-ships or links, to the possible number.

did not correlate significantly with the ranking of the estates on $\overline{Y\text{-}Y'}$. However, the ranking of the mean number of children under five years did correlate significantly at the 5 % level. This is not altogether surprising since it correlated initially with gross activity. It would tend to suggest that while the number of children was in some way accounted for in the regression as a component in the two variables of age and work situation, part of its explanatory power was not accounted for. It is interesting that social class again failed to prove influential. The ranking of the estate means on social class correlated very poorly with the $\overline{Y\text{-}Y'}$ ranking.

Thus the general occupational level of an estate population would not appear to affect its activity–deviance. There was only one other variable in this group of means which produced a significant rank correlation coefficient and that was the mean estate attitude to newcomers. (This rank correlation coefficient was significant at the 5 % level.) From the consideration of this group of variables it can be concluded that, wherever there is an accumulation on an estate of either a large number of children under school-age or housewives who profess a favourable attitude to new neighbours, one might expect the general level of activity on that estate to exceed expectation.

Turning now to the second group of variables; the correlation of the rankings of standard deviations, or homogeneity indices, produced two significant results. When the ranking of the standard deviation of the number of children on the estate under the age of five was compared with the activity-deviance ranking, it yielded a highly significant value of $r_s = 0.9520$. It would appear from this, that heterogeneity in the number of young children possessed by the estate families is conducive to a level of activity in excess of expectation. The estate ranking on the standard deviation of social class also correlated significantly with activity-deviance. This fact suggests that homogeneity of social class on an estate encourages visiting, regardless of the general social-class level on that estate.

When the estate ordering on each of the three sociometric indices was related to activity-deviance a significant correlation was found in each case; the side-neighbour and clique indices were significant at the 1 % level and the mutual pairs index at the 5 % level. It was this result in particular, which suggested the most fruitful course for further investigation.

THE RANKING ANALYSIS – SUMMARY AND CONCLUSIONS

It had been hypothesised that activity-deviance would be explained by those characteristics of the physical environment such as the site layout, that had been determined by the planner, builder or architect. The ranking procedure which was adopted to test this hypothesis, showed that this was not the case. However, two further findings of the ranking analysis suggested where the source of the explanation of mean activity-deviance might lie. First, there was a close association between the estate rankings on activity-deviance, $\overline{Y-Y'}$, and each of the three sociometric indices. There was also a close association between the estate rankings on the sociometric indices and on $\overline{Y}$. As one might expect in the light of this last finding, the estate rankings on $\overline{Y}$ and $\overline{Y-Y'}$ were also highly correlated. This suggested that whatever factors explained the magnitude and ranking of the sociometric indices, would also explain the estate rankings on $\overline{Y}$ and $\overline{Y-Y'}$. Second, the significant correlation between the ranking on estate activity-deviance and the ranking on both the mean number of young children and their distribution, suggested that some function of the demographic composition of the estate might explain why the activity level on one estate exceeded the 'normal' and why it fell below this level on another. Thus it seemed logical to seek the explanation for the magnitude of the sociometric indices and *ipso facto*, for sociometric linkage, in the demographic characteristics of the linked individuals themselves.

The rationale for such a procedure is as follows. The regression analysis had indicated the level of the individual's visiting potential. Whether this potential was achieved would obviously depend upon whether or not the individual had established at least one personal relationship. (Such an assumption was verified by the proven relationship between the sociometric indices and the estate ranking on $\overline{Y-Y'}$.) Therefore, in order to explain activity-deviance or the under- or over-achievement of this potential, it was necessary to discover under what circumstances each relationship had been formed: in other words, to discover what factors had determined the attraction of the individuals concerned.

It might be suggested that attraction and repulsion, liking and disliking, would be determined by psychological, rather than demographic factors. However, as stated earlier, to study the psychological characteristics of the people who were interviewed, was beyond the scope of this research. Furthermore, there was a potent argument for examining the demographic characteristics of the linked individuals, in order to discover what had attracted them to each other. The psychological characteristics of an individual only become apparent over a period of continual contact. On new housing estates, it is unlikely that the residents will have had sufficient time to discover the psychological characteristics of their fellows. The early social interaction with which this study is concerned, is more likely to be based on outwardly-visible signs of perceived compatibility, namely on demographic similarity.

In order to explain the ranking of the estates on activity-deviance, it was necessary to explain their ranking on the sociometric indices. However, the magnitude of these indices depended upon the extent to which social relationships had been established. This being so, only when the reasons for relationship formation are understood, can any conclusions be made concerning the ranking of the estates on activity-deviance. To this end, the approach that was adopted was to compare the demographic characteristics of visiting individuals.

The sociometric analysis

THE DATA

The sociometric data in this study were derived from the visiting data. For each respondent, it consisted of those persons whom she had visited at least once in the preceding month. A second criterion was also used. This was to ensure that if extenuating circumstances had prevented the respondent from making any visits in the previous month, there would be some indication of whom she might have been expected to visit had the situation been normal. This second set of data was derived from the respondent's reply to the question, 'Which of the estate members do you feel you know well enough to call on?'

The conformity of the data from these two sources was measured by an index of concordance developed for such a purpose by Katz and Powell.[1] The calculation of this index is explained in Appendix VI where the estate indices have also been listed. It was found that the index of concordance was at least significant at the 5% level for each of the eight estates. This agreement between the two sociometric criteria was felt to validate the first one, namely the 'persons visited' criterion.

THE DEFINITIONS

The definitions which were used in the sociometric analysis are as follows. If an individual A visited a second B at least once in the given time period, a 'sociometric link' was said to exist between them and their relationship was defined as a non-reciprocal or one-way relationship. However, if B also visited A at least once in that time, the relationship was then defined as a reciprocal, a mutual or a two-way relationship. If a mutual relationship existed between each pair of persons of a group of *n* persons, a true clique of these *n* members was said to exist.

THE MATRIX MANIPULATION PROCEDURE

The existence of mutual relationships was established by constructing a visiting matrix for each of the eight estates and deriving from this, the symmetrical matrix. (The symmetrical matrix refers to mutual relationships only.) By successively squaring and cubing the symmetrical matrices, true 3-person cliques were identified. To illustrate this operation, the sets of matrices for two of the eight estates have been included in this book (see Appendix VI). They refer to the Skilbeck and Grasmere estates. The former had few sociometric links while the latter was an estate with a highly developed network of visiting relationships. The sociograms for these and the other six estates, have also been included in Appendix VI and allusion will be made to these, later in the text. Table 23 summarises the results of the matrix manipulation.

[1] L. Katz and J. H. Powell, 'A Proposed Index of Conformity of One Sociometric Measurement to Another', in J. L. Moreno, *The Sociometry Reader*, Free Press of Glencoe, 1960, pp. 298–306.

TABLE 23 *A summary of the results of the matrix manipulation*

Estate	No. non-reciprocal relationships	No. mutual pairs	No. true 3-person cliques	No. respondents
Whitmarsh	27	56	11	47
Aston	16	33	12	34
Huntley	6	13	1	24
Garton	5	11	1	16
Grasmere	10	17	12	12
Skilbeck	1	2	0	9
Utting	3	6	1	8
Church Close	5	0	0	8
TOTAL	73	138	38	158

It could be argued that mutual pairs and true cliques could be identified more easily by inspecting the sociogram for any particular estate, thereby avoiding the lengthy operation of successively powering matrices. However, the sociograms for the larger estates are far too complex to make cursory inspection a reliable means of identifying all the relationships of any given type.[1] Powering the matrices guarantees that no relationship will be overlooked.

While the work of raising the symmetrical matrices beyond the third power was not felt to be justified, reference to the structure of the 3-person cliques, revealed the few larger cliques. On the Grasmere estate, one 5-person clique was traced, consisting of the respondents at houses numbered 2–6 inclusive. On Jersey Close, Aston, two 4-person cliques were found, although they had three common members, namely the respondents at 3, 8 and 9; the housewives at 6 and 10 were the fourth members.

RELATIONSHIP FORMATION AND DEMOGRAPHIC COMPATIBILITY

The marked discrepancy between even estates of similar size in the number of sociometric links which had been formed, added further weight to the argument, expressed earlier in this chapter, for investigating the causal nature of the constitution

[1] See for example, the Whitmarsh sociogram in Appendix VI.

of the social group. It was important to discover why relationships did, or did not, exist so that some conclusion could be drawn on the reasons for the greater or lesser degree of relationship formation on the different estates. Only when this was achieved, could the ordering of estates on activity-deviance be explained.

The causality investigation was designed to test the hypothesis that the individuals who participated in a reciprocal visiting relationship would be more likely to be matched on significant characteristics than participators in a non-reciprocal relationship: and that the latter in their turn would be more likely to be matched than the non-visiting pairs. In other words, there would be an association between the strength or intensity of a relationship and the demographic compatibility of the individuals concerned.

To this end, all social relationship on each estate were classified according to their intensity, i.e. as reciprocal, non-reciprocal or non-visiting. These relationships were then divided into the ones involving matched and the ones involving unmatched individuals. For this matching process, each related pair was compared on six characteristics. Their age group and work situation was compared, the number of children under five years which each had and whether or not each possessed at least one child in the same age group.[1] Such individual and family characteristics could all have been established by an interested observer and therefore might well have been used by a potential interactor as criteria for assessing compatibility. However, two further characteristics were examined. While these would only have become apparent to participators after contact had been established, they had appeared in the regression and in consequence it was felt that their role should be examined in this context. These characteristics were the geographical mobility expectation of each individual and whether each had extended help to a newcomer. In order to test the hypothesis that there was an association between the intensity of relationships and the demographic compatibility of the

---

[1] The age groups of the children corresponded approximately to the divisions imposed by our educational system, namely 0–4, 5–10, 11–15, and 16–21 years respectively.

participants, the data for the separate estates was combined.

The tables showing the association between the intensity of their relationships and the matching of the participating individuals on each of the 6 characteristics, can be seen in Appendix VII. When a chi-square test was performed on the six sets of data, it was found that there was a highly significant tendency for a relationship to be formed, and particularly a reciprocal relationship, between individuals who were in the same age-group and between mothers who each had a child in the same age group. (In each case, the value of chi-square was significant at the ·005 level.) There was an indication that the actual number of reciprocal relationships in which each of the participating individuals had given help to a newcomer significantly exceeded expectation. However, this difference was only just significant at the 5% level. For the other characteristics, the work situation, the number of young children and the mobility expectation, the observed frequencies did not differ significantly from the expected ones. Thus, on these new housing estates, there was a strong tendency for visiting relationships to be formed between housewives who were of a similar age or who had children in the same age group.

However, the reader might argue that side-neighbours, regardless of their demographic compatibility, would enter into visiting relationships with each other. To discover whether the convenience of proximity compensated to any extent for compatibility, all the relationships were divided into two groups. The first group contained the relationships between side-neighbours and the second group, the relationships between non-neighbours. Then the analysis of the effect of matching was repeated but this time on each group separately. The results of the chi-square tests performed on the six sets of data for the side-neighbour relationships and for the non-neighbour relationships are also to be found in Appendix VII. It can be seen from this that the analysis of side-neighbour relationships only yielded one significant value of chi-square, and this only at the 5% level. It referred to the compatibility of age. An examination of the relevant table showed that there was a tendency for reciprocal visiting relationships to exist between side-neighbours who were in the same age group. However, the observed number of non-reciprocal relationships in which the pair were matched on age, fell below expectation. This tends to suggest that some effort is made to form, and sustain relationships with adjacent neighbours, regardless of perceived compatibility; but the stronger relationships, as indicated by their reciprocal nature, result from, or are supported by, similarity of age.

It could be argued that while people feel under an obligation to remain friendly with their immediate neighbours for the comfort of all concerned, relationships with other estate members are entered into on a more voluntary basis. If this was the case on the study estates and compatibility was thought to be desirable in a relationship, one would expect to find that the relationships between non-neighbours would be more likely to be characterised by matching than those between side-neighbours. This indeed proved to be the case. There was a significant tendency for non-neighbour relationships, particularly reciprocal ones, to be based on the possession of a child in the same age group, as well as on similarity of age. (The chi-square values for the two relevant distributions being significant at the 0·5 % and 5 % levels respectively.)

Thus the general conclusion that visiting relationships were likely to be based on demographic compatibility, can be slightly modified. Those visiting relationships which require some physical effort to establish were more likely to be based on demographic compatibility than those which were facilitated by close proximity.

VISITING LEVELS AND DEMOGRAPHIC COMPATIBILITY

It will be recalled that explaining sociometric linkage was only an intermediate step in explaining the ranking of the estates on $\overline{Y-Y'}$ and $\overline{Y}$. It was the visiting activity of the individual estate members which determined the estate means for Y and $Y-Y'$. Therefore, the explanation of the individual levels of activity and activity-deviance was a prerequisite to the explanation of the estate levels, and thence of their ordering. It was shown above that there was a strong tendency for visiting relationships to develop between individuals who shared certain characteristics. But it is now necessary to show that an association also existed between the number of visits exchanged by linked individuals and their compatibility on these characteristics.[1] Taking the study population as a whole, it was found that a total of 890 visits were exchanged between individuals who were either of a similar age or had a child in the same age group, or both, while only 336 visits were made between individuals who were matched on neither characteristic. The conclusion here is self-evident. The situation at the individual level can be assessed from Table 24. This shows the visiting frequency according to whether or not donor and recipient were matched. Again, 'matched' implies similarity of age in either the participants or their children, or both.

TABLE 24 *The frequency of visiting and the matching of the participating individuals*

No. visits made by donor	Matched %	Unmatched %	TOTAL %	No.
		Recipients who were		
1	58·88	41·12	100	197
2	63·41	36·59	100	41
3	77·78	22·22	100	9
4	68·63	31·37	100	51
5 or more	80·39	19·61	100	51
TOTAL				349

Two points arise from the table. First, regardless of their frequency, visits were more likely to be extended to matched, rather than unmatched individuals. This confirms the findings of the sociometric analysis reported above. Second, as the frequency of visiting increased, the chance that the participating individuals were matched, also increased. There is an unequivocal association then, between the amount of visiting within a relationship and the demographic similarity of the individuals concerned.

PHYSICAL CONSTRAINTS ON RELATIONSHIP FORMATION

From the foregoing discussion, one might be forgiven for concluding that relationships between similar individuals on each estate occurred spontaneously. Obviously some form of social

[1] It must be remembered that the number of visits within a particular relationship, say y, is not necessarily equal to Y but only contributes to it, inasmuch as $y_1 + y_2 + \ldots + y_n = Y$, where an individual is linked to n others.

contact between them must have occurred to provide them with the opportunity of selecting compatible others. As stated in Chapter 1, Festinger and Merton both suggested that the opportunity for such contact from which social relationships could develop, was circumscribed by the physical environment. They found that an individual is more likely to establish friendship links with the people living nearest to her and with those whose dwellings are orientated towards her own. In order to determine whether these conclusions are valid in the heterogeneous population under consideration here, it is necessary to show two things. First, if the proximity thesis applied, there should be an inverse relationship between distance and the total number of sociometric links. Second, if the orientation of the dwellings exerted a significant influence, there should have been a greater tendency for sociometric links to be established between those side-neighbours in houses with facing doors, compared with the side-neighbours who had no such facility for inevitable physical contact.

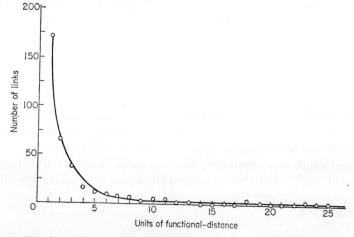

Fig. 2 Total number of sociometric links by functional distance

The graph in figure 2, shows that an inverse relationship between sociometric linkage and distance certainly existed in the study population. To ensure that the data for all the estates was comparable, the distance between dwellings was measured in 'units of functional-distance', one unit representing the distance between houses which were either adjacent or opposite each other.[1] It is clear from the graph that taking the study population as a whole, visiting relationships were more likely to be formed with the people who lived nearby. For instance, there were almost three times as many links between people living one unit of functional-distance apart, compared with those living two units apart. Nevertheless, it is important to notice that relationships had been formed over considerable distances. Three sociometric links even existed over a functional-distance of 23 units. This willingness to overcome distance in order to find 'suitable' friends, will be referred to again later.

An examination of the situation on individual estates, provides further evidence of Festinger's inverse relationship. Table 25 indicates how the proximity influence operated on each estate. It can be seen that on six out of the eight estates, at least 50 % of all the sociometric links were formed with people living only one unit of functional-distance away.

Examining the influence exerted by dwelling orientation on the formation of visiting relationships, it was found that, contrary to expectation, proportionately fewer links were established between side-neighbours with facing doors, compared with side-neighbours with no facing doors. The relative distribution of links between the two groups can be seen in Table 26. However, the difference between the two groups was only small and when a chi-square test was performed on the frequency data, this difference proved to be non-significant.

Thus while there was no conclusive evidence that in the study population the orientation of the dwellings significantly influenced relationship formation, proximity unquestionably did. In order to discover whether proximity also influenced the activity level within these relationships, the association between proximity and actual visiting levels will now be considered.

---

[1] The connotation of the term 'functional-distance' is the same as in the term 'physical-functional-distance' employed earlier in this chapter. It applies to the distance along the conventional route joining the relevant dwellings. Thus, even if the rear-gardens of two dwellings backed on to each other, the functional-distance between these dwellings would be measured according to the foot-path route. This usage can be justified on the basis that while visual contact between such people is easy, it is visiting contact that is the important criterion here and functional-distance must therefore measure the effort required for visiting.

TABLE 25   *The percentage distribution on each estate of the sociometric links according to the functional-distance between the linked individuals*

Estate	% of links by units of functional-distance					TOTAL	
	1	2	3	4	5 or more	%	No. links
Whitmarsh	41·01	21·58	9·35	6·48	21·59	100·00*	139
Aston	50·00	19·51	12·20	1·22	17·08	100·00*	82
Huntley	59·38	9·38	6·25	—	25·00	100·00*	32
Garton	62·96	18·52	3·70	—	14·81	100·00*	27
Grasmere	45·45	18·18	15·91	6·82	13·64	100·00	44
Skilbeck	80·00	—	20·00	—	—	100·00	5
Utting	60·00	20·00	13·33	6·67	—	100·00	15
Church Close	60·00	—	20·00	20·00	—	100·00	5
TOTAL							349

* Where the total is not quite 100%, this is due to rounding errors.

TABLE 26   *The influence of dwelling-orientation on sociometric linkage*

Side-neighbours with	% of possible links that were		TOTAL	
	Realised	Unrealised	%	No.
Doors facing	46·30	53·70	100·00	54
No doors facing	50·45	49·55	100·00	122
TOTAL				176

PHYSICAL CONSTRAINTS ON VISITING LEVELS

The relationship between the total number of visits and the distance between donor and recipient can be seen from figure 3. There is an unmistakable trend here. Over half of all the visits that were made in the study population were extended to people living either next-door or opposite, i.e. at a functional-distance of one unit. The number of visits diminishes sharply with an increase in distance.

Table 27 shows how the frequency of visiting was related to distance. In spite of cell-merging due to small frequencies, a

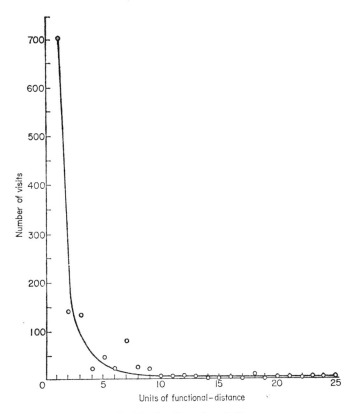

Fɪɢ. 3 Total number of visits by functional-distance

comparison of the observed and expected (bracketted) frequencies reveals two trends. There was a tendency for only single visits to be made to people who lived beyond the immediate environment. Also, where frequent visiting occurred, it was more likely to be with individuals who lived close at hand. It is important to realise that this does not imply that visiting with next-door neighbours was necessarily frequent. Rather, it suggests that *where* there was an inclination to visit the next-door neighbour frequently, proximity facilitated such interaction.

Thus, as well as influencing relationship formation, proximity also affects the frequency of the visiting within those relationships.

TABLE 27 *Visiting frequency by functional-distance*

| No. visits | Units of functional-distance | | | TOTAL |
	1	2	3 or more	
1	80 (95·97)	45 (36·69)	72 (64·35)	197
2	26 (19·95)	4 (7·63)	11 (13·39)	41
3 or more	64 (54·08)	16 (20·68)	31 (36·26)	111
TOTAL	170	65	114	349

Chi-square= 13·09   At P=0·025 when v=4, chi-square=11·4

The reconciliation of the regression and sociometric analyses

The regression model, in defining the individual's visiting potential, could be said to also define her motivation to visit. In order to satisfy this visiting potential the individual must enter into visiting relationships. But in order to form such relationships, it is necessary for her to make contact with people whom she considers 'suitable'. The sociometric analysis has shown that the 'suitable' individuals are those who are demographically similar to herself and the opportunity of meeting them is conditioned by their proximity. Once the individual has established one or more relationships, the amount of visiting within each relationship is also determined by proximity and demographic similarity. Therefore, it seems likely that for any particular individual, her success or failure in fulfilling her visiting potential depends upon the presence and location on her estate of similar individuals. If similar people are only to be found at a distance, it seems probable that her actual activity, Y, will at most be approximately equal to her predicted activity, Y'. Only when similar individuals are situated close at hand, will Y tend to exceed Y' to any significant extent.

If this reasoning is correct, the estates which are high on the ranking of activity-deviance, $\overline{Y-Y'}$, will be those that are so constituted that similar individuals are grouped together. This does not necessarily imply that the whole estate must be demographically homogeneous.[1] It means rather, that where there

[1] Indeed, it was found that the estate ranking on the homogeneity of age (as measured by the standard deviation of age) was poorly correlated with the estate ordering of $\overline{Y-Y'}$.

has been a chance agglomeration of similar individuals, they are likely to intervisit sufficiently to exceed their potentials. This would naturally have the effect of producing a high estate value for $\overline{Y\text{-}Y'}$.

An examination of the sociograms in relation to individual values for $Y\text{-}Y'$, showed that this reasoning was correct. For the sake of brevity only three sociograms will be discussed here. They refer to the Grasmere, Huntley and Church Close estates, representing respectively, estates of high, medium and low ranking on $\overline{Y\text{-}Y'}$. Their sociograms can be seen in Appendix VI.

The Grasmere estate ranked second on $\overline{Y\text{-}Y'}$. It illustrates admirably the thesis that when similar individuals are grouped together, relationships will form between them that will lead to activity in excess of expectation. The housewives at 2, 3, 4, 5 and 6 were all of a similar age and each had young children. Not only did relationships develop between them (they constituted a true 5-person clique) but the visiting that resulted was such that $Y\text{-}Y'$ was positive for each of them. Proximity had indeed reinforced similarity as an instigator and sustainer of social activity. On the other hand, the young respondent at 11 also had a young child. Yet after one year of occupation she had only established one reciprocal, and one non-reciprocal relationship with the members of the clique[1] at the top of the Close, despite the fact that they were demographically similar to her. In consequence, her actual visiting level fell considerably below her expected level. The fortuitous juxtaposition of the middle-aged housewives at 1, 8, 9 and 10, provided them with the opportunity of meeting each other and of forming visiting relationships based on compatibility of age. While they did not remain an exclusive group, intervisiting between them did occur and each of them exceeded her predicted visiting level. Festinger would probably have argued that the respondent at 12, being a physical isolate, would remain a social isolate too. However, it is suggested here that she would have been unlikely to form any social relationships on the estate wherever she had been situated, since she was the only elderly person living there.

[1] This term is used in the sociometric rather than the pejorative sense.

The Huntley and Church Close estates which were fifth and seventh respectively in the ordering of $\overline{Y-Y'}$, each contained families at widely varying life-stages. They differed however, in one critical respect. The Huntley estate was large enough with 24 occupied dwellings, to contain several families at each particular life-stage. On the other hand, the Church Close estate with only eight houses was not thereby offering its housewives enough opportunity of finding others demographically similar to themselves with whom they could exchange visits. As a result, few sociometric links were observed on the Church Close estate, despite its compact shape which might appear ideal for promoting social activity. Therefore, it is hardly surprising that the actual visiting level of only two out of the eight Church Close respondents surpassed the predicted level. For the remaining six, $Y-Y'$ was both high and negative.

The Huntley estate shows how the chance distribution of similar families affected relationship formation. Where homogeneous grouping occurred, interaction developed. But where similar families were widely spaced, the phenomenon was virtually absent.[1] For example, the three old-aged pensioners at 4 and 6 Pasture Lane and 3 Oakham Close were near enough to each other for visual contact to be inevitable. On the basis of their similarity of age, relationships of mutual aid and regular visiting developed between them with the result that their scores on activity-deviance were positive and high. However, visual contact between these three respondents and the other two elderly respondents on the estate, at 8 and 12 Oakham Close, was more random. There was no evidence that the physical barrier of distance separating them had been overcome in order to establish visiting relationships. In consequence, the activity-deviance scores of these two individuals proved to be negative.

For the rest of the Huntley estate, there was a marked tendency for visiting to involve side-neighbours only. Wherever reciprocal relationships between side-neighbours were based on similarity of age, the participating individuals exceeded their visiting potentials. But where age differences between side-

[1] The respondents at 9 Oakham Close and 8 Hawthorne Road were the only exceptions.

neighbours prevented either any relationship development or intensive visiting within the relationship that did form, the individuals concerned tended to under-achieve, failing to reach their potentials.

While this discussion has focussed on the situation on only three estates, the choice of these three was somewhat arbitrary. Any of the other five could just as easily have illustrated the contentions examined above. *What is clear, is that the estates with a high ranking on $\overline{Y-Y'}$ were those on which chance had clustered together housewives who were either similar in age, or who had children at the same stage.* On the medium-ranked estates, some grouping of homogeneous housewives had occurred. At the same time, there were significant numbers of housewives who were segregated from similar others. The low-ranking estates were so heterogeneous in composition that each respondent tended to be a social isolate. The implications of these findings for planning policy generally, will be considered in the last chapter.

5 The Conclusion

When approximately 350,000 new dwellings are built each year in England and Wales, there is a strong case for asking what principles underlie the planning and construction of these homes. Architects and town planners openly admit that when designing an estate they are primarily concerned with practical and aesthetic considerations. To them the all important factors are such things as the final appearance of the estate and whether the traffic will flow smoothly around it. The effect of their design on the social lives of the future residents receives little attention. However, one cannot blame them for their failure to take into account the social implications of their planning; the literature survey in Chapter 1 showed that there has been much confusion in sociological research over the exact nature of the influence of planning factors on social behaviour.

It was the intention of this study to discover the influence, if any, planning factors exerted on the social activity on new owner-occupied housing estates. The quantitative technique which was used in this research had the advantage that it also included an analysis of the influence which characteristics of the residents themselves had, on the social activity of the estates. There were three principal findings of the research; these will be summarised before their implications for planning practice are discussed.

The principal findings

First, from the many personal characteristics which previous workers had suggested as determinants of individual activity rates, only five proved to exert a significant influence when incorporated in a regression model.[1] These were: the individual's age, her geographical mobility expectation, whether she went out to work, whether she had a relation living on the estate, or whether she had given help to a new neighbour during the early days of estate life. When these five variables were combined to predict individual activity rates, their predictive power was found to be on the low side despite being very significant statistically. The proportion of individual activity which could be predicted from the regression model containing these five variables, was only 27·8 %.

Second, it had been hypothesised that the activity unaccounted for by the regression would be explained by the physical features of the estate. A ranking method was employed to test this hypothesis. It was found that neither the overall layout of the estate, nor its size, nor the spacing of the dwellings, could explain this residual activity. Similarly, neither the general price-level of the homes, nor even the degree of variety of house-type, could account for the activity which the regression had failed to predict. Thus, contrary to the expectations based on the findings of Festinger, Merton, and others, these particular planning variables failed to influence the mean level of activity-deviance on the eight estates examined. In response to this failure, closer attention was paid to the sociometric data. It was felt that the ultimate explanation for residual activity might lie in the mechanism by which visiting relationships were formed.

The results of this sociometric analysis constitute the third major finding of the study. The level of the residual activity on each housing estate depended upon the distribution over the estate of demographically similar families. It was discovered that on these heterogeneous private estates there were two components to relationship formation. These were proximity and demographic similarity. Furthermore, the frequency of visiting was also found to be related to these two factors. Thus, for relationships to be characterised by frequent visiting it was

---

[1] Undoubtedly, the restriction of this research to women, was to be regretted. Earlier workers, in treating the respondent as the unit of study, were able to later break down the responses by sex.

necessary for the individuals concerned to be living close to each other and either to be of a similar age, or to have children of a similar age[1] or both. Thus an individual's actual activity rate would not only depend upon her visiting 'potential', or the extent to which she exhibited those five characteristics that the regression analysis had shown determined activity levels, it would also depend upon the opportunity she had of satisfying this potential. This opportunity was circumscribed by the demographic composition of her estate and by the location of individuals who were demographically similar to herself. This being so, it was a logical step to examine the demographic composition and distribution of each estate to discover whether this was the key to explaining the ranking of the estates on mean residual activity (or activity-deviance). This proved to be so. The estates on which the individuals tended to over-achieve[2] and estate activity-deviance was positive, were indeed the estates on which demographically similar individuals were situated close to each other. The estates on which most of the individuals under-achieved, and where estate activity-deviance was nega-tive, the housewives had experienced difficulty in finding people of the same age as themselves, or with children of similar ages, with whom to exchange visits. Their difficulty could be attri-buted to the fact that people of similar demographic circum-stances either were widely scattered over the estate, or were not to be found there at all. Thus, for an estate to be characterised by social activity in excess of expectation, it should be composed of groupings of demographically homogeneous families. For general social activity to be high, a further condition needs to prevail. The estate should be populated largely by people with a high visiting potential, as defined by the regression model.

The implications of these findings for planning policy

This study has been based on the supposition that social inter-

---

[1] It may seem strange that the presence of children proved to be a potent ex-plainer of residual activity although the children variable did not appear in the regression model. The reason for this is to be found in the fact that the children variable was covariant with the two variables of age and work situation, both of which were incorporated in the regression model.

[2] An individual 'over-achieves' when she visits at a level in excess of her 'potential'.

course between the residents of new housing estates is a desirable end in itself. For planners who accept this, the conclusions of this research suggest two respects in which they might promote social intercourse.

First, houses of a type which will be particularly attractive and well suited to families at a given life-stage, might be situated together on an estate, rather than scattered arbitrarily over that estate. This does not imply that all estates should consist of identical houses; rather that the houses of a similar appeal should be grouped together.

Second, the grouping of similar houses might be planned in such a way as to facilitate contact between the residents. For this purpose, the houses need not necessarily be built close together, but easy visual contact, which could lead to social contact, should be possible. It could be that to this end, houses arranged around a 'turning' would be more suitable than in a ribbon.

The Whitmarsh estate illustrates well how the failure of the planners to appreciate these two fundamental issues affected the social life of its residents. The four-bedroomed houses had indeed been scattered arbitrarily over the estate. Having four bedrooms, they were more likely to appeal to families with more than two children. Also, being more expensive than the three-bedroomed houses, a purchaser of one of these larger houses might well have been a little older than the purchaser of a three-bedroomed house. These factors could suggest that the house-wives in the larger houses would have more in common with each other than with their neighbours in the smaller houses. The sociogram for the Whitmarsh estate shows that relationships had been formed between the respondents in some of the four-bedroomed houses despite the distance between them. The respondents' accounts of how their relationships developed indicated that chance alone brought them together. However, frequent contact between them was hindered by the distance separating them. Had the four-bedroomed houses been situated closer together, initial contact would have been inevitable, not relying on chance alone, and visiting could have been more frequent.

Another feature of the social life on the Whitmarsh estate

illustrates the importance of the second implication for planning policy, namely, that similarly planned houses, when grouped together, might be sited so as to facilitate visual contact. The two-bedroomed bungalows, which were clearly best suited to small households, were all situated on Dorchester Close. Because they were sited along one side of the road and, furthermore, because they were staggered, visual contact between the residents was difficult. In consequence, although four elderly respondents lived in the bungalows, no visiting relationships had been established between them. There would seem to have been a strong case for arranging the bungalows around the closed end of the cul-de-sac – the 'turning' – where visual contact would have been almost inevitable.

In the private housing market, it is impossible in the final analysis to dictate how an estate will be populated. But it has been shown in this work that the judicious planning of an estate can indeed influence the social lives of the people who live there.

APPENDIX I

Schedule A

THE UNIVERSITY OF KEELE

UNIT IN STATISTICAL SOCIOLOGY

*A Study of Inter-Family Relationships
on New Estates*

Estate ....

House number

Road .... and/or name...

1. What is your name? ....

2. (a) Do you have any children?
    Yes   No
   (b) IF YES: How many of them live at home?
    0   1   2   3   4   5   6   ....

Name of Child	Sex	Age
1	M F	....
2	M F	....
3	M F	....
4	M F	....
5	M F	....
6	M F	....

   (c) CHECK Am I right in thinking these are all of your
       children?
       Yes   No
       IF NO: Ask Question 12.

3. Is there anyone else in the household?
    Yes   No

Name	Sex	Relationship to Respondent
1	M F	....
2	M F	....
3	M F	....

   CHECK   So there are .... of you altogether?

4. When did you move into this house?
    Month.. Year 196.............

5. (a) Where did you live before you came here?
         ....

    (b) Did you own that house/flat/bungalow?
         Yes   No

6. Why did you move from there?
    Wanted to own a house...1
    Wanted a larger house...2
    Husband's job..3
    Recently married...4
    To be near relatives...5
    Other (STATE)
        6
        7
        8

7. (a) HUSBAND'S OR PRINCIPAL EARNER'S OCCUPATION
         Could you tell me what kind of work your husband
         does?
         Occupation ....
         Firm ....
         Industry ....
    (b) How does he travel to work?
         Car   Bus   Train   Bicycle   Walks

8. WIFE'S WORK
    (a) Do you go out to work?
         Full-time 1
         Part-time 2
         No...3
    (b) IF 1 or 2: What is your job?
         Occupation ....
         Firm ....
         Industry ....
    (c) How do you travel to work?
         Car   Bus   Train   Bicycle   Walks

9. (a) Do either/any of you happen to have a car?
    Yes   No
    (b) IF YES   How many cars have you?
        1   2

10. WIFE'S PLACE OF ORIGIN
    (a) Do you think of...as your home town?
        i.e. the place where you were brought up.
        Yes   No
    (b) IF NO   Where?
        Native town...
    (c) Do your parents live there now?
        Yes   No
    (d) IF NO   Where do they live?
        Parents' home town ....

11. HUSBAND'S PLACE OF ORIGIN
    (a) Does your husband also come from...?
        Yes   No
    (b) IF NO   Which is his home town?
        Husband's native town..
    (c) Do his parents live there now?
        Yes   No
    (d) IF NO   Where do they live?
        Parent's home town ....

12. (a) Have you any children living elsewhere?
        Yes   No
        (b) IF YES   Where do they live?
                    Name   Town
        1 ....
        2 ....

13. FAMILY ACTIVITIES
    (a) Do you go to any club or association where you might
        meet people from the estate? (SHOW LIST. ENTER BELOW)
        REPEAT FOR HUSBAND AND CHILDREN
    (b) Is there a local club that you would be interested in
        joining once you have settled in? (ENTER BELOW)
        REPEAT FOR HUSBAND AND CHILDREN

H

(c)　Have you any other leisure pursuits that take you away from your home? e.g. evening classes, week-end pursuits.
REPEAT FOR HUSBAND AND CHILDREN

	Wife	*Husband*	Children			*Other* (SPECIFY)
			1	2	3	
Membership						
Desired Membership						
Other leisure pursuits						

14.　Do you think that the people on this estate are friendly?

Very
friendly　　Friendly　　Don't
know　　Unfriendly　　Very
unfriendly

15.　(a)　Did you know anyone on the estate before you moved in?

Yes　　No

　　(b)　IF YES　Who?

　　　　　　　Name　　　　　　　　　　　　Address

　　　1 ....　　...

　　　2 ....　　...

　　　3 ....　　...

16.　(a)　When you were moving in, did anyone offer you any help or hospitality in a neighbourly spirit, i.e. more positive than just passing the time of day?

Yes　　No

　　(b)　IF YES　Who?

　　　　　　　Name　　　　　　　　　　　　Address

　　　1 ....　　...

　　　2 ....　　...

　　　3 ....　　...

17. (a) Have you been invited into anyone else's house on the estate?
    Yes   No
    (b) IF YES   Whose house?
              Name   Address
        1 ....
        2 ....
        3 ....
    (c) Do you recall how this happened?
        1 ....
        2 ....
        3 ....

18. (a) Have you invited anyone on the estate into your home?
    Yes   No
    (b) IF YES   Who?

		Name	Address	With husband	With children
For tea/coffee	1	....	....	....	....
	2	....	....	....	....
	3	....	....	....	....
For a meal	1	....	....	....	....
	2	....	....	....	....
	3	....	....	....	....
Other reason	1	....	....	....	....
	2	....	....	....	....
	3	....	....	....	....

Estimated Age of Respondent: Date of Interview ....
20–29.................................1
30–39.................................2
40–49.................................3
50–59.................................4
60 or over 5

THE UNIVERSITY OF KEELE
RESEARCH UNIT IN STATISTICAL SOCIOLOGY

*A Study of Inter-Family Relationships
on New Estates*

Estate .... Address ....

INFORMATION CHECK

| SCHEDULE A INFORMATION | ALTERATIONS |

Name ....
No. of Children........................... ....
No. Adults ....
Husband's
Occupation ....
   Firm ....
   Mode Travel ....
Wife's Occupation......................... ....
   Firm ....
   Mode Travel ....
   Full-time/Part-time   Full-time/Part-time
Car ownership............................... ....
Club Membership and Frequency:

Wife	....	C O	....	C O
	....	C O	....	C O
	....	C O	....	C O
Husband	....	C O	....	C O
	....	C O	....	C O

Children........................... ....

....
Wife's Parents'
Home ....
Husband's Parents'
Home ....

Other Children's
Home ....

....

Date of Occupation..
1. How often do you see your relatives?
   More than   About once   Every ....   Every ....
   once a week   a week   weeks   months

Wife's
Parents   ....
Husband's
Parents   ....
Other
(SPECIFY)   ....

   ....

2. Which estate members do you feel you know well enough
   to call on?
   1.............................. S OP O   5.............................. S OP O
   2.............................. S OP O   6.............................. S OP O
   3.............................. S OP O   7.............................. S OP O
   4.............................. S OP O   8.............................. S OP O

3. Have you visited any of these people or others on the
   estate, in the *last month?* Who? How many times? Were
   you invited or did you call for some other reason? At what
   time of the day did you go? Did your husband accompany
   you?

	Reason for visit				
Person visited	*If invited*	*Other*	*Time*	*Husband*	
....	....	....	D E	Yes	No
....	....	....	D E	Yes	No
....	....	....	D E	Yes	No
....	....	....	D E	Yes	No
....	....	....	D E	Yes	No
....	....	....	D E	Yes	No
....	....	....	D E	Yes	No
....	....	....	D E	Yes	No

....	....	....	D E	Yes	No
....	....	....	D E	Yes	No
....	....	....	D E	Yes	No

4. Have any of the estate members visited you in the last month? Who? How many times? Did you invite them or did they call for some other reason? At what time of the day did they come? Did their husbands come too?

	Reason for visit			
Visitor	If invited	Other	Time	Husband
....	....	....	D E	Yes No
....	....	....	D E	Yes No
....	....	....	D E	Yes No
....	....	....	D E	Yes No
....	....	....	D E	Yes No
....	....	....	D E	Yes No
....	....	....	D E	Yes No
....	....	....	D E	Yes No
....	....	....	D E	Yes No
....	....	....	D E	Yes No

5. Do either you or your husband, or both of you, go out with anyone from the estate? With whom? Where? How often?

	Name	Frequency	Place	Persons involved
1	....	....	....	W H B
2	....	....	....	W H B

6. Since you moved into this house, have you become friendly with anyone else in ....? Yes No
IF YES Do you recall how you first met?

	Friend	Road	Occasion of first meeting
1	....	....	....
2	....	....	....
3	....	....	....

7. (a) Have you visited her/them in the last month?

Yes No

IF YES How many times?

1 .... 2 .... 3 ....

(b) Has she visited you in the last month?   Yes   No
IF YES   How many times?
1 ....   2...............................   3...............................

8. Apart from the people you have already mentioned to me, do you have any other friends whom you visit? Yes   No
IF YES   Where are they living now?   How often do you manage to visit them?

	Present residence	*Frequency*	*Present residence*	*Frequency*
1			3	
2			4	

9. Do you have any special friend or friends on the estate or elsewhere in.., with whom you would try to keep in touch if either of you moved away?   Yes   No
IF YES   Do you think there was any particular reason why you became close friends?   (PROMPT IF NECESSARY)

	Friend	*Location*	*Reason*
1		E O	
2		E O	
3		E O	
4		E O	

10. I believe you moved from...
Was that the only town you had lived in since your marriage?
Yes   No
IF NO   In what other towns have you lived?
1 ....   3...
2 ....   4...

11. If your husband changed his job, is it likely that you would have to move away from here?
Yes   Possibly   No

12. If for any reason you did move, is there any aspect of the estate that you would be sorry to leave?
Yes   No
IF YES   What?

....

....

13. Do you think that you will be moving in the next 12 months?
    Yes   D.K.   No

14. Which attitude do you think a person should take to a new neighbour?
    (SHOW LIST)
    1   2   3   4   5

15. Which attitude do you think most people round here take?
    1   2   3   4   5

16. (a) Is there any feature of this house that you particularly like?
    Yes   No
    IF YES   What?

    ....

    (b) Is there anything that you dislike?
    Yes   No
    IF YES   What?

    ....

17. It has been said that houses should be designed so that the occupants have as much privacy as possible. Do you agree?
    Strongly   No definite   Strongly
    agree   Agree   feelings   Disagree   disagree

18. Do you think that this house gives you enough privacy? Why?
    Yes   Now   No
    Reason...

19. Do you feel that you are close enough to:
    (a) Shops? ....   Yes   No
    (b) Schools? ....   Yes   No
    (c) Other (STATE) ....   Yes   No

20. Do you think that there is adequate provision for enter-
tainment in ....?
Yes   No
IF NO   What would you like to see here?

....

....

Alone/Husband present   M/A/E   Date.....................
Position of external doors: F/S/B

SUPPLEMENTARY SHEET FOR NEW OCCUPANTS

1. When did you move into this house?......................196......

2. Where did you live before you came here?........................

3. Did you own that house?   Yes   No

4. Why did you move from there?..

   ....

5. Where do you think of as your native area? i.e. the place
   where you were brought up........................

6. And your husband's native area?........................

7. Do you think that the people on this estate are friendly?
   Very   Don't   Very
   friendly   Friendly   know   Unfriendly unfriendly

8. Did you know anyone on the estate before you moved in?
   Yes   No
   IF YES   Who?

   ....

   ....

9. When you were moving in, did anyone offer you any
   help or hospitality in a neighbourly spirit? i.e. more positive than just passing the time of day.
   Yes   No
   IF YES   Who?

   ....

   ....

10.   IF THE RESPONDENT IS A REPLACEMENT:
Do you happen to know why the previous owners left?

....

Estimated age: 20–29..............................1
30–39..............................2
40–49..............................3
50–59..............................4
60 or over...................5

APPENDIX II

The Site-Plans (Scale 1:2,500 approx.)

Note: For the purpose of this study, the houses on the Skilbeck and Grasmere estates have been renumbered.

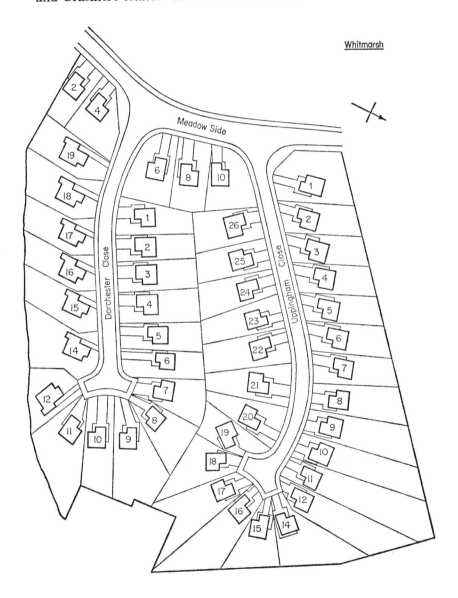

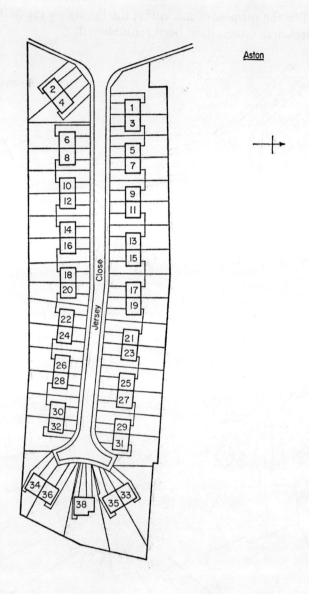

Aston

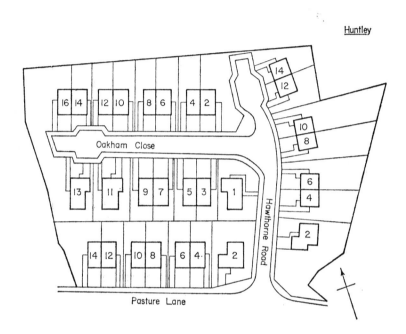

Huntley

Oakham Close

Hawthorne Road

Pasture Lane

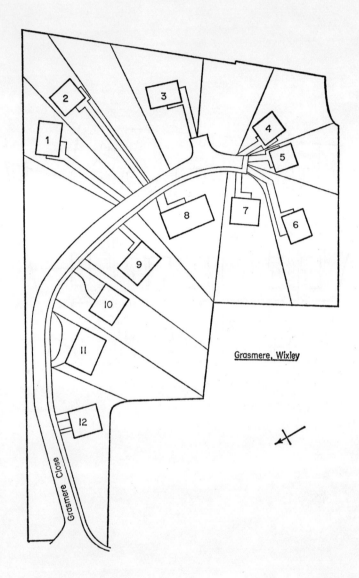

Grasmere, Wixley

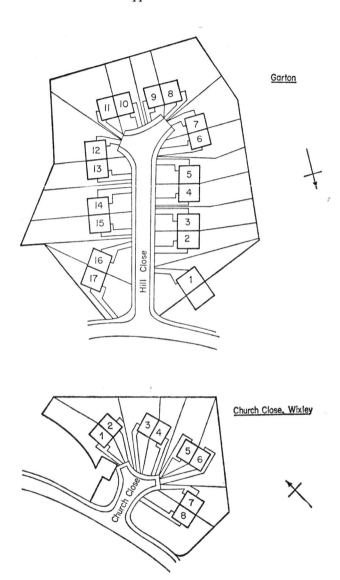

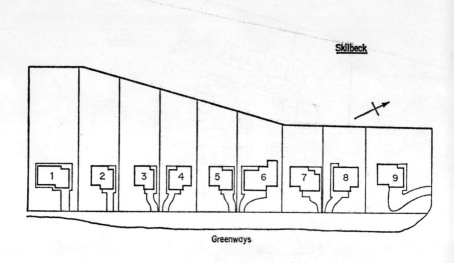

Skilbeck

Greenways

Utting

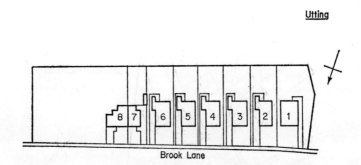

Brook Lane

APPENDIX III

The Transformation of Y

The skewed distribution of the raw data in *Y* (see figure 4) was

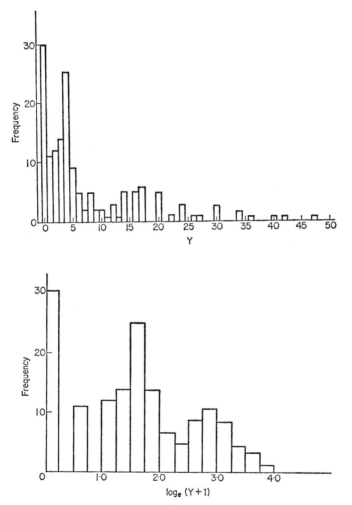

FIG. 4 Frequency distribution of the number of estate visits made by respondents before transformation (above) and after transformation (below).

I

unacceptable for two reasons. First, when an analysis of variance is performed on data which is not normally distributed, it is likely that the variances within each class will be related to the mean of that class, thereby affecting the validity of the F-test.[1] Second, the use of the correlation techniques which were to be

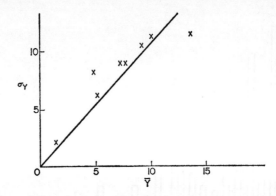

FIG. 5 Relationship between the standard deviation of Y and the mean of Y on 8 estates. Fitted line: $\sigma_Y = 0 \cdot 027 + 1 \cdot 067_Y$

employed in this study is based on the assumption of normality.[2] Therefore, it was neccessary to find a method which would transform Y to normality while simultaneously stabilising the variance.

It can be seen from Figure 5 that the class (estate) standard deviations in Y proved to be proportional to the class means in Y. This relationship suggested that a natural logarithmic transformation would make the variances independent of the means.[3] The shape of the distribution of the raw data again suggested a natural logarithmic transformation.[4] The existence of zero Y values invalidated the $\log_e Y$ transformation, demanding instead, $\log_e(Y+1)$. Accordingly, this transformation was tried. Because Bartlett's test for the homogeneity of the variance[5] and

[1] Snedecor and Cochran, *op. cit.*, pp. 276–7, 325.
[2] *ibid.*, p. 185.
[3] *ibid.*, pp. 329–30.
[4] M. H. Quenouille, *Introductory Statistics*, Butterworth-Springer, 1950, pp. 164–5.
[5] Snedecor and Cochran, *op. cit.*, 296–8.

a chi-square goodness of fit test[1] indicated that the transformation had proved satisfactory by meeting both requirements, the $\log_e(Y+1)$ transformation was adopted. The distribution of $\log_e(Y+1)$ can be seen in Figure 4.

The Independent Variables

The 23 independent variables on which the regression analysis was based, are listed below. For convenience, they have been divided into five groups. These groups consist of the demographic variables, the mobility variables, the attitudinal measures and those variables that are concerned with extra-estate activity and intra-estate experience respectively. For 22 of these, information is provided on the way in which it was measured, its frequency distribution over the study population and where applicable, the transformation which was employed to normalise its distribution. The twenty-third variable, as explained below, is the quadratic term in social class. The first variable on the list, age, will be discussed in more detail than the succeeding ones to illustrate the procedure which was adopted in preparing each variable for the regression analysis.

I THE DEMOGRAPHIC VARIABLES

(i) *Age*

Measure: The respondent's age was estimated to fall within one of the following five categories:—20–29, 30–39, 40–49, 50–59 years or 60 years and over.

Frequency distribution: *J*-shaped with the maximum frequency for the youngest age group.

Transformation: $1/X$ It can be seen from figure 6, that the frequency distribution for the raw data on age was very highly skewed. Therefore, it required a powerful transformation. A number of reciprocal transformations were tried, e.g. $1/(X+0.5)$ and $1/(X+0.25)$. However, the transformation $1/X$ was found to approximate most nearly to normality when a chi-square goodness of fit test was applied to the transformed data. It was then necessary to test this transformation

[1] *ibid.*, pp. 84–5.

for linearity with transformed Y. This was achieved by fitting a polynomial of the second degree to the data and testing the contribution made to this regression by the linear and quadratic terms.[1] It can be seen from the resulting analysis of

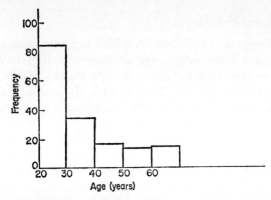

FIG. 6 Frequency distribution of age for 158 respondents.

variance (see Table 28), that the improvement due to the quadratic term was not significant. Therefore, a linear relationship was assumed between the transformed variables of age and activity.

TABLE 28   *Analysis of variance for testing the linear regression of activity upon Age*

Source of variation	Sum of squares	Degrees of freedom	Mean Square	F
Variation due to linear term	9·6639	1	9·6639	8·5032
Extra variation due to quadratic term	0·0526	1	0·0526	0·0463
Total variation due to regression	9·7165	2	—	—
Residual variation	176·1551	155	1·1365	
TOTAL	185·8716*	157		

* The slight discrepancy in the value for the total sum of squares as recorded here and in Table 20, is attributable to the fact that these preliminary operations were performed on a desk calculator while the step-wise regression was performed on a computer.

[1] Quenouille, *op. cit.*, pp. 127–31.

(ii) *Number of Children under 5 years of age*

Measure: The total number of children under 5 years of age possessed by the respondent.

Frequency distribution: J-shaped with maximum frequency at 0 children.

Transformation: $1/(X+1)$ Because data was available for each respondent on both the number and the age of her children, it was possible to establish whether merely the possession of at least one child in a given age group as measured by a dummy variable or their actual number, bore the strongest relationship to transformed Y. Accordingly, each of the possible variables was correlated with transformed Y. It will be seen from Table 29 that the actual number of children under 5 years of age produced the highest correlation. Hence, this variable was used in the regression analysis.

TABLE 29 *Correlation coefficients with transformed Y*

Age-group of children years	Correlation coefficient when the variable is	
	Number of children in the age-group	*Possession of children in the age-group (dummy)*
0–4	—0·2138*	0·1974
0–11	0·1997	0·1825
0–20	0·1847	0·1736

* This variable required a reciprocal transformation thereby producing a value of *r* with a sign contrary to expectation.

(iii) *Social Class*

Measure: The respondent's social class was assessed according to her husband's occupation or if she was unmarried, according to her own occupation The Hall-Jones scale of occupational prestige for males[1] was used to classify these occupations. This provided a 7-point scale with class 1 containing the occupations of highest prestige and class 7, the occupations of highest prestige and class 7, the occupations of lowest prestige.

[1] J. Hall and D. Caradog Jones, 'Social Grading of Occupations', *Brit. J. Sociol.*, vol. I. (1950), pp. 31–55. See also A. N. Oppenheim, *Questionnaire Design and Attitude Measurement*, Heinemann, 1966, pp. 275–84.

Frequency distribution: Slightly positively skewed and ranging over classes 1–6 only.

Transformation: $1/(X+0.5)$ A second-degree polynomial produced a significantly better fit with transformed Y than a first-degree one. Therefore, it was necessary to represent social class by two variables in the regression analysis. These were the linear and squared terms respectively.

(iv) *Work Situation of the Respondent*

Measure: Dummy variable: $1 =$ works outside the home; $0 =$ does not work outside the home.

The definition of part-time work was difficult because a considerable amount of variation was found in the number of hours worked by the part-timers in the study population. Therefore, the original plan to allow for part-time work as well as full-time work by using an ordered dummy variable, was modified, to be replaced by the dichotomy.

II THE MOBILITY VARIABLES

(i) *Past Geographical Mobility*

Measure: The total number of homes, including the present one, in which the respondent had lived during her married life.

Frequency distribution: Positively skewed.

Transformation: $\log_e (1/X) + 1$

(ii) *Distance from Origin*

Measure: Distance in miles from the respondent's native town, i.e. the place where she was brought up.

Frequency distribution: J-shaped with maximum frequency in the $0-0.99$ miles class.

Transformation: $1/\sqrt{(X+3)}$

(iii) *Distance of the Last Move*

Measure: Distance in miles from the respondent's previous home.

Frequency distribution: J-shaped with maximum frequency in the $0-0.99$ miles class.

Transformation: $1/(X+4)$

(iv) *Tenure of Previous Home:*

Measure: Dummy variable: $1 =$ owned previous home; $0 =$ did not own it.

(v) *Future Geographical Mobility Expectation*

Measure: Ordered dummy variable derived from the answer to the question, 'If your husband changed his job, is it likely that you would have to move away from here?' Coding of responses: 0 = no; 1 = possibly; 2 = yes.

III ATTITUDINAL MEASURES

(i) *Attitude to New Neighbours*

Measure: The social distance scale used by Fellin and Litwak in their studies at Detroit and Buffalo,[1] i.e. the responses to the question, 'Which attitude do you think a person should take to a new neighbour?'

Coding of responses:

1 = Go over after the move and offer help.

2 = Go over after the move and introduce yourself, but give help only if asked.

3 = Don't go unless invited but be friendly.

4 = Don't be too friendly until you see what kind of people they are.

5 = Stay away from newcomers and keep to existing friends.

Frequency distribution: Positively skewed.

Transformation: $\log_e X$

(ii) *Attitude to Privacy*

Measure: Likert-type scaling of a single item.

Item: 'It has been said that houses should be designed so that the occupants have as much privacy as possible.'

Coding of responses:

1 = Strongly agree; 2 = Agrees; 3 = No definite feelings; 4 = Disagree; 5 = Strongly disagree.

Frequency distribution: Positively skewed.

Transformation: $1/(X+1)$

IV EXTRA-ESTATE ACTIVITY VARIABLES

(i) *Visits to Relations*

Measure: Total number of visits in the previous month to relations living outside the estate.

Frequency distribution: *J*-shaped with bunching and maximum frequency at 0 visits.

[1] Fellin and Litwak *op. cit.*, p. 373.

Transformation: $\log_e(X+1)$

(ii) *Visits to Friends*

Measure: Total number of visits in the previous month to friends living outside the estate.

Frequency distribution: Positively skewed.

Transformation: $\log_e(X+1)$.

(iii) *Membership of Social Clubs*

Measure: Total number of local social clubs to which respondent belonged. ('Local' clubs being the ones at which it would have been possible to meet other estate members.)

Frequency distribution: J-shaped with maximum frequency at 0 clubs.

Transformation: $1/(X+1)$.

(iv) *Number of Cars*

Measure: Total number of cars in respondent's household.

Frequency distribution: Slightly positively skewed.

Transformation: —

V INTRA-ESTATE EXPERIENCE VARIABLES

(i) *Relative on the Estate*

Measure: Dummy variable: 1 =Has a relative living elsewhere on the estate; 0 =Does not have a relative on the estate.

(ii) *Proportion of the Estate Occupied on Arrival*

Measure: The proportion of the estate that was occupied when the respondent took up residence. (The 'full' estate was defined as the number of dwellings that were occupied at the Stage II interviews.)

Frequency distribution: Approximately normal.

Transformation: —

(iii) *Received Help*

Measure: Dummy variable: 1 =Received help from another estate member when first moved onto the estate; 0 = Received no help.

(iv) *Gave Help*

Measure: Dummy variable: 1 =Gave help to a newcomer to the estate; 0 =Gave no help.

(v) *Length of Residence*

Measure: Number of months between occupation and the Stage II interviews.

Frequency distribution: Slightly positively skewed.

Transformation: $\sqrt{X}$

(vi) *Adequacy of Privacy*

Measure: Dummy variable: 1 = This house gives us enough privacy; 0 = This house does not give us enough privacy. (The respondents who felt that, because they had taken precautions, e.g. by erecting fences, they *now* had enough privacy, were classified in the '1' category.)

(vii) *Sentiments for the Estate*

Measure: The number of aspects of the estate that the respondent said she would be sorry to leave if she moved away.

Frequency distribution: Positively skewed.

Transformation: $\log_e(X+1)$

TABLE 30   Matrix of Simple Correlation Coefficients between the Respondent and Independent Variables

Variable		1	2	3	4	5	6	7	8	9	10	11	12
Estate visits	1		0·2424	0·0113	−0·0132	−0·0315	0·0630	0·0900	0·2388	−0·1390	0·3349	0·2163	0·0162
Age	2			0·1600	−0·0531	0·3191	0·0738	−0·0422	0·2761	0·2156	0·1157	0·0528	0·0157
No. social clubs	3				0·1432	0·1385	−0·1881	0·0835	−0·1583	0·0922	0·0751	−0·1571	0·0789
Att. to new neighrs	4					0·1573	−0·0883	0·2161	−0·0426	0·0561	0·0292	−0·0840	0·0089
Visits to relations	5						0·0736	0·1693	−0·0771	0·1495	0·0685	−0·0724	0·1023
No. feats sry to lve	6							0·0218	0·0367	0·0553	0·0445	0·1231	0·0996
Length of residence	7								−0·0342	0·0657	0·0150	−0·0569	0·0977
Geog. mobility exptn	8									0·0639	−0·0782	0·2216	−0·0893
Work situation	9										0·1310	−0·1518	0·1736
Relation on estate	10											−0·0019	0·0845
No. cars	11												−0·0829
Adequacy of privacy	12												
Received help	13												
Gave help	14												
Previous ownership	15												
Social class (X)	16												
Social class (X²)	17												
Distance of move	18												
Distance from origin	19												
Propn est. occupied	20												
No. homes	21												
Attitude to privacy	22												
No. chn under 5 yrs	23												
Visits to friends	24												

Variable		13	14	15	16	17	18	19	20	21	22	23	24
Estate visits	1	-0.0602	0.1668	0.1096	0.0624	0.0528	-0.0827	-0.0551	-0.1657	-0.0320	-0.0676	-0.2138	0.1381
Age	2	0.0744	-0.1008	-0.4072	-0.2069	-0.2138	0.0837	0.0681	0.0649	0.5546	-0.1429	-0.1925	0.1374
No. social clubs	3	-0.0165	0.0872	-0.2608	-0.4642	-0.4154	0.0944	0.2274	-0.0039	0.2271	-0.1033	-0.0887	-0.2059
Att. to new neighrs	4	-0.0527	0.0055	-0.1319	-0.1449	-0.1005	0.1645	0.2039	-0.1350	0.1350	0.0049	0.0197	-0.1963
Visits to relations	5	-0.0160	-0.0330	-0.3053	-0.3919	-0.3330	0.3335	0.5510	-0.0448	0.3490	-0.1297	0.0074	0.2162
No. feats sry to lve	6	0.0841	0.0574	0.0288	-0.0805	-0.1114	-0.0924	-0.0254	0.0114	0.0564	0.0188	-0.0231	0.1095
Length of residence	7	-0.2568	0.2611	-0.0606	-0.1674	-0.1159	0.1475	0.2633	-0.6994	-0.0174	0.0358	-0.0323	-0.0460
Geog. mobility exptn	8	0.1093	-0.0515	0.0084	0.3821	0.3281	-0.2206	-0.2879	-0.0616	-0.0057	0.0284	-0.2055	-0.0070
Work situation	9	0.0776	-0.1937	-0.4324	-0.2125	-0.1672	0.1811	0.3260	0.0745	0.3625	-0.0024	0.3696	0.0944
Relation on estate	10	-0.0553	-0.0460	-0.0781	-0.2012	-0.1704	0.2057	0.2675	0.0264	0.0412	-0.0129	0.0888	0.0059
No. cars	11	0.0671	-0.0008	0.2233	0.3223	0.2743	-0.1351	-0.1991	-0.0085	-0.1514	0.0705	-0.1600	0.0438
Adequacy of privacy	12	0.1260	-0.1256	-0.1071	-0.0936	-0.0460	0.2425	0.1603	0.0514	0.0375	-0.2757	0.1368	0.0722
Received help	13		-0.1791	-0.0496	0.1253	0.1074	-0.1179	-0.0772	0.2612	0.0108	-0.0777	0.1387	0.0687
Gave help	14			0.2767	-0.0261	-0.0546	-0.1026	-0.0777	-0.3617	-0.1499	-0.0344	-0.0722	0.0535
Previous ownership	15				0.1984	0.1424	-0.1290	-0.1946	-0.0036	-0.4815	-0.0325	-0.2035	0.0163
Social class (X)	16					0.9703	-0.2781	-0.5038	-0.0020	-0.3751	0.0786	-0.0261	0.1005
Social class (X²)	17						-0.1804	-0.4154	0.0014	-0.3238	0.0757	0.0246	0.0747
Distance of move	18							0.5990	0.1627	0.2177	-0.1306	0.0667	0.0527
Distance from origin	19								0.0109	0.3446	-0.1218	0.1517	0.0727
Propn est. occupied	20									0.1106	-0.0401	0.0874	0.0721
No. homes	21										-0.1027	0.2571	-0.0613
Attitude to privacy	22											0.0249	-0.1039
No. chn under 5 yrs	23												0.0718
Visits to friends	24												

APPENDIX V

TABLE 31   *The analysis of variance of the regression residuals $(Y-Y')$*

Source of variation	Sum of squares	Degrees of Freedom	Mean square	F
Between estates	7·4700	7	1·0671	1·2630
Within estates	126·7379	150	0·8449	
TOTAL	134·2079	157		

At P=0·05 with 7 and 150 degrees of freedom, F=2·07
Conclusion: The variation between estates on $Y-Y'$ is not significantly greater than the variation within estates on $Y-Y'$.

The Comparison of Estate Means on $Y-Y'$

The standard error of the difference between the ith. and kth. class means, with unequal n, is given by[1]:

$$\sqrt{\frac{s_i^2}{n_i}+\frac{s_k^2}{n_k}}$$

The difference between the ith and kth class means is significant at the 5 % level, if the difference exceeds the product of the standard error of the difference and $t_{0·05}$, with $(N-a)$ degrees of freedom, where a is the number of classes.[2]

For the Study data, with $(158-8)=150$ degrees of freedom, $t_{0·05}=1·96$. The tables below, indicate respectively, the critical and the actual values of the difference between each pair of estate means on $Y-Y'$, calculated according to the principles set out above.

TABLE 32   *The critical value at the 5% significance level, of the difference between each pair of estate means on $Y-Y'$*

Estate	Utting	Gras- mere	Whit- marsh	Aston	Huntley	Garton	Church Close	Skil- beck
Utting		0·6101	0·5153	0·5506	0·5827	0·5386	0·7468	0·8659
Grasmere			0·4857	0·5229	0·5568	0·5104	0·7266	0·8487
Whitmarsh				0·4083	0·4508	0·3920	0·6486	0·7832
Aston					0·4908	0·4375	0·6772	0·8069
Huntley						0·4773	0·7036	0·8293
Garton							0·6676	0·7989
Church Close								0·9516
Skilbeck								

[1] Snedecor and Cochran, *op. cit.*, pp. 278–9.
[2] *ibid.*, pp. 271–2.

TABLE 33 *The actual difference between each pair of estate means on Υ- Υ'*

Estate	Utting	Gras-mere	Whit-marsh	Aston	Huntley	Garton	Church Close	Skil-beck
Utting		0·4914	0·6853	0·7521	0·7574	1·0697	1·4651	1·6461
Grasmere			0·1939	0·2607	0·2660	0·5783	0·9737	1·1547
Whitmarsh				0·0668	0·0721	0·3844	0·7798	0·9608
Aston					0·0053	0·3176	0·7130	0·8940
Huntley						0·3123	0·7077	0·8887
Garton							0·3954	0·5764
Church Close								0·1810
Skilbeck								

TABLE 34 *The Spearman Rank Correlation Coefficient between estate means on Υ-Υ' and other variables*

Variable		r_s	Significance level
$\overline{Υ}$		0·9520	0·01
$\overline{Υ'}$		−0·3094	n.s.
Estate Planning Features			
Size		0·1440	n.s.
Hailing-distance	(mean)	0·3333	n.s.
Physical-functional-distance	(mean)	0·2858	n.s.
Purchase-price of dwellings	(mean)	0·2619	n.s.
Purchase-price of dwellings	(standard deviation)	0·2160	n.s.
Respondent Characteristics I	(means)		
Age		−0·1667	n.s.
Work situation		0·1920	n.s.
No. children under 5 years		0·8520	0·01
Geographical mobility expectation		0·0714	n.s.
Relation on the estate		0·3298	n.s.
Age of all children on estate		−0·4522	n.s.
Social class		−0·0714	n.s.
Duration of residence		−0·0238	n.s.
Attitude to new neighbours		0·6428	0·05
Attitude to privacy		0·2640	n.s.
No. cars		−0·2142	n.s.
No. social clubs		0·1190	n.s.
No. homes		0·1429	n.s.

TABLE 34—*cont.*

Variable	r_s	Significance level
Respondent Characteristics II (standard deviations)		
Age	0·3094	n.s.
Work situation	0·1200	n.s.
No. children under 5 years	0·9520	0·01
Age of all children on estate	−0·6188	n.s.
Social class	0·6905	0·05
Duration of residence	−0·2618	n.s.
Attitude to new neighbours	−0·2618	n.s.
Attitude to privacy	0·4762	n.s.
Sociometric Indices		
Mutual pairs index	0·8048	0·05
Side-neighbour index	0·9520	0·01
Clique index	0·8520	0·01

Critical values of r_s when $N=8$: (two-tailed test)

5% significance level, $r_s=0·643$
1% significance level, $r_s=0·833$

APPENDIX VI

The Measurement of the Extent of Agreement between the Two Sets of Sociometric Data

THE INDEX OF CONFORMITY

The index of conformity was designed to measure the extent of agreement of the data of one sociometric test with another test made either at a different time or on another test criterion.[1] In other words, it should answer the question, 'To what extent does the occurrence of relation Y in the ordered pairs, conform to the occurrence of relation X?'

The index of conformity $\hat{y}$ is defined as:

$$\hat{y} = \frac{1}{n_x n_{\bar{y}}} \left[n(n-1)n_{xy} - n_x n_y \right]$$

where for an ordered pair:

n refers to the number of cases in which the relations exist.

$x, \bar{x}, y$ and $\bar{y}$ refer respectively to the existence of relation X, the non-existence of relation X, the existence of relation Y and the non-existence of relation Y.

THE INDEX OF CONCORDANCE

When neither X nor Y can be defined as the dependent relation, the index of conformity is used to define an index of concordance between the two sociometric tests. The coefficient of concordance, C, is defined as the geometric mean of the two indices of conformity, $\hat{y}_1$, and $\hat{y}_2$, of X with Y and Y with X. i.e.

$$C^2 = \hat{y}_1 \, \hat{y}_2$$

THE USE OF THE INDICES ON THE STUDY DATA

Since neither the 'people visited' criterion nor the 'people known well enough to call on' criterion could be defined as the dependent relation, $\hat{y}_1$, was calculated with 'people visited' as the dependent relation and $\hat{y}_2$ was calculated with 'people known well enough to call on' as the dependent relation. The results of these calculations appear overleaf.

[1] Katz and Powell *op cit.* pp. 298-306

TABLE 35

Estate	Indices of conformity		Coefficient of concordance (C)
	$\hat{\gamma}_1$	$\hat{\gamma}_2$	
Whitmarsh	0·7829	0·7171	0·7492
Aston	0·6629	0·6455	0·6542
Huntley	0·4596	0·8265	0·6163
Garton	0·6533	0·6262	0·6396
Grasmere	0·5667	0·5862	0·5764
Skilbeck	0·1173	1·0000	0·3426
Utting	0·3171	0·5608	0·4216
Church Close	0·2941	1·0000	0·5423

SIGNIFICANCE TEST

It was possible to use the chi-square test of significance on the coefficients of concordance since:

$$C^2 = \frac{\chi^2}{n(n-1)}$$

Result: The coefficient of concordance was at the least, significant at the 5% level for each estate.

SKILBECK

Visiting Matrix

Visited

Visitor	1	2	3	4	5	6	7	8	9	
1										0
2			1							1
3		1				1				2
4					1					1
5				1						1
6										0
7										0
8										0
9										0
	0	1	1	1	1	1	0	0	0	5

SKILBECK—*cont.*

Symmetrical Visiting Matrix

Visited

		1	2	3	4	5	6	7	8	9	
	1										0
	2			I							1
	3		I								1
	4					I					1
Visitor	5				I						1
	6										0
	7										0
	8										0
	9										0
		0	1	1	1	1	0	0	0	0	4

Squared Symmetrical Visiting Matrix

Visited

		1	2	3	4	5	6	7	8	9	
	1										0
	2		I								1
	3			I							1
	4				I						1
Visitor	5					I					1
	6										0
	7										0
	8										0
	9										0
		0	1	1	1	1	0	0	0	0	4

K

Appendix VI

Cubed Symmetrical Visiting Matrix

Visited

		1	2	3	4	5	6	7	8	9	
	1										
	2			I							0
	3		I								I
	4					I					I
Visitor	5				I						I
	6										0
	7										0
	8										0
	9										0
		0	I	I	I	I	0	0	0	0	4

GRASMERE, WIXLEY

Visiting Matrix

Visited

		1	2	3	4	5	6	7	8	9	10	11	12	
	1		I		I			I						3
	2	I		I	I	I	I	I						6
	3		I		I	I	I							4
	4	I	I	I		I	I					I		6
	5		I	I	I		I							4
Visitor	6	I	I	I	I	I		I						6
	7							I						1
	8	I	I							I				3
	9	I				I			I			I		4
	10	I			I	I				I				4
	11	I			I	I								3
	12													0
		7	6	4	7	7	5	1	3	2	0	2	0	44

Symmetrical Visiting Matrix

Visited

Visitor	1	2	3	4	5	6	7	8	9	10	11	12	
1		1		1				1					3
2	1		1	1	1	1		1					6
3		1		1	1	1							4
4	1	1	1		1	1					1		6
5		1	1	1		1							4
6		1	1	1	1		1						5
7						1							1
8	1	1							1				3
9								1					1
10													0
11				1									1
12													0
	3	6	4	6	4	5	1	3	1	0	1	0	34

Squared Symmetrical Visiting Matrix

Visited

Visitor	1	2	3	4	5	6	7	8	9	10	11	12	
1	3	2	2	1	2	2		1	1		1		15
2	2	6	3	4	3	3	1	1	1		1		25
3	2	3	4	3	3	3	1	1			1		21
4	1	4	3	6	3	3	1	2					23
5	2	3	3	3	4	3	1	1			1		21
6	2	3	3	3	3	5		1			1		21
7		1	1	1	1		1						5
8	1	1	1	2	1	1		3					10
9	1	1							1				3
10													0
11	1	1	1		1	1					1		6
12													0
	15	25	21	23	21	21	5	10	3	0	6	0	150

Appendix VI

Cubed Symmetrical Visiting Matrix

Visited

	1	2	3	4	5	6	7	8	9	10	11	12	
1	4	11	7	12	7	7	2	6	1		1		58
2	11	16	16	18	16	17	3	9	1		4		111
3	7	16	12	16	13	14	3	5	1		3		90
4	12	18	16	14	16	17	3	5	2		6		109
5	7	16	13	16	12	14	3	5	1		3		90
6	7	17	14	17	14	12	5	5	1		3		95
7	2	3	3	3	3	5		1			1		21
8	6	9	5	5	5	5	1	2	3		2		43
9	1	1	1	2	1	1		3					10
10													0
11	1	4	3	6	3	3	1	2					23
12													0
	58	111	90	109	90	95	21	43	10	0	23	0	650

Visitor

THE SOCIOGRAMS

Key

———— Reciprocal relationship

.......→ Non-reciprocal relationship

Excluded from the study population

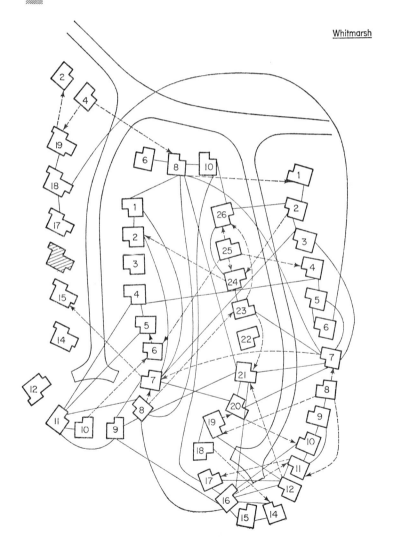

Whitmarsh

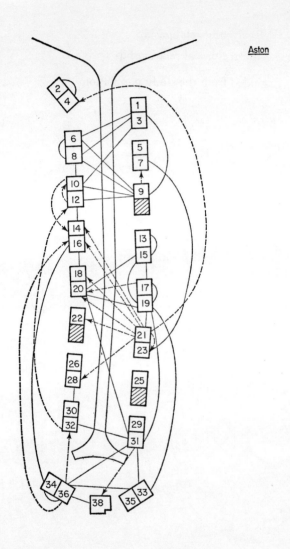

Aston

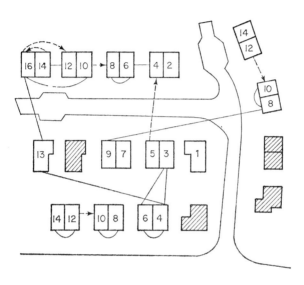

Huntley

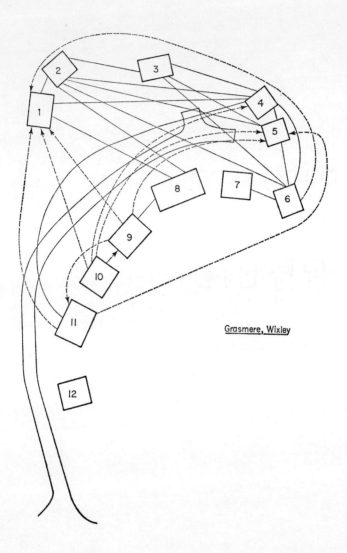

Grasmere, Wixley

Garton

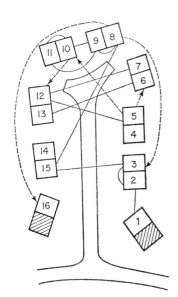

Church Close, Wixley

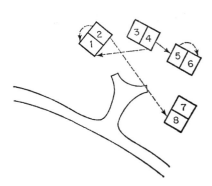

Skilbeck

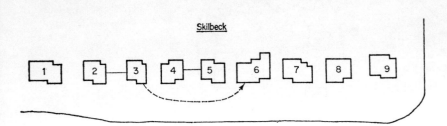

Utting

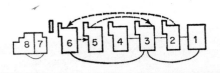

APPENDIX VII

The Effect of Common Characteristics on the Development of Visiting Relationships

I AGE

Type of Relationship	No. relps. in which the participants are		TOTAL
	Same age	Different age	
Reciprocal	70 (51·07)*	68 (86·93)	138
Non-reciprocal	29 (26·96)	44 (46·04)	73
Non-visiting	713 (733·97)	1272 (1251·03)	1985
TOTAL	812	1384	2196

Chi-square = 12·33
At P = 0·005, with 2 degrees of freedom, chi-square = 10·60.
* The figures in brackets are the expected frequencies.

II AGE OF CHILDREN

Type of relationship	No. relps. in which the participants have		TOTAL
	Children of the same age	No children of the same age	
Reciprocal	55 (25·98)	83 (112·02)	138
Non-reciprocal	19 (13·71)	54 (59·29)	73
Non-visiting	339 (373·31)	1646 (1611·69)	1985
TOTAL	413	1783	2196

Chi-square = 46·33
At P = 0·005, with 2 degrees of freedom, chi-square = 10·60.

III GAVE HELP

Type of relationship	No. relps. in which		TOTAL
	Both participants gave help	One or neither participant gave help	
Reciprocal	32 (22·20)	106 (115·80)	138
Non-reciprocal	9 (11·72)	64 (61·28)	73
Non-visiting	312 (319·08)	1673 (1665·92)	1985
TOTAL	353	1843	2196

Chi-square = 6·10
At P = 0·05, with 2 degrees of freedom, chi-square = 5·99

IV WORK SITUATION

| Type of relationship | No. relps. in which the participants have | | TOTAL |
	Same work situation	Different work situation	
Reciprocal	90 (81·20)	48 (56·80)	138
Non-reciprocal	44 (42·87)	29 (30·13)	73
Non-visiting	1157 (1166·93)	828 (818·07)	1985
TOTAL	1291	905	2196

Chi-square=2·59
At P=0·05, with 2 degrees of freedom, chi-square=5.99

V GEOGRAPHICAL MOBILITY EXPECTATION

| Type of relationship | No. relps. in which the participants have | | TOTAL |
	Same mobility expectation	Different mobility expectation	
Reciprocal	64 (57·62)	74 (80·38)	138
Non-reciprocal	30 (30·41)	43 (42·59)	73
Non-visiting	822 (827·97)	1163 (1157·03)	1985
TOTAL	916	1280	2196

Chi-square=1·30
At P=0·05, with 2 degrees of freedom, chi-square=5·99

VI NUMBER OF CHILDREN UNDER 5 YEARS OF AGE

| Type of relationship | No. relps. in which the participants have | | TOTAL |
	Same no. children under 5	Different no. children under 5	
Reciprocal	21 (13·08)	117 (124·92)	138
Non-reciprocal	6 (6·91)	67 (66·09)	73
Non-visiting	181 (188·01)	1804 (1796·99)	1985
TOTAL	208	1988	2196

Chi-square=5·72
At P=0·05, with 2 degrees of freedom, chi-square=5·99

The Effect of Common Characteristics on the Development of Visiting Relationships when the Participants are:
1 Side-neighbours
2 Non-neighbours

1 *Side-neighbour Relationships*

Common characteristic	Value of chi-square	Significance-level
Age	6·47	0·05
Age of children	1·06	n.s.
Gave help	1·55	n.s.
Work situation	2·29	n.s.
Geographical mobility expectation	2·31	n.s.
Number of children under 5	3·00	n.s.

2 *Non-neighbour Relationships*

Common characteristic	Value of chi-square	Significance-level
Age	7·01	0·05
Age of children	48·82	0·005
Gave help	5·99	0·05
Work situation	4·83	n.s.
Geographical mobility expectation	1·04	n.s.
Number of children under 5	1·24	n.s.

At P=0·05 with 2 degrees of freedom, chi-square=5·99
At P=0·005 with 2 degrees of freedom, chi-square=10·60

BIBLIOGRAPHY

ARMOUR, S. J. *Introduction to Statistical Analysis and Inference for Psychology and Education*, Wiley, 1966.

BEAVER, S. H. 'The Potteries: A Study in the Evolution of a Cultural Landscape', *Inst. Brit. Geog. Trans. & Papers*, 1964, no. 34.

BELL, C. 'Mobility and the Middle Class Extended Family'. *Sociology*, vol. 2, no. 2 (1968), pp. 173–84.

BELL, C. *Middle Class Families*, Routledge, 1968.

BOTT, E. *Family and Social Network*, Tavistock 1968 (first publ. 1957).

BRACEY, H. E. *Neighbours*, Routledge 1964.

BROADY, M. 'Social Change and Town Development', *Town Planning Rev.*, vol. 36, no. 4 (1966), pp. 269–78.

BUILDING SOCIETIES ASSOCIATION 'Analysis of Home Loans made by Building Societies during October 1964', *Building Society Statistics*, no. 6 (special issue Apr. 1965).

COOPERATIVE PERMANENT BUILDING SOCIETY 'Who Buys Houses? (1968)', *Occasional Bulletin*, no. 87, Oct. 1968.

CULLINGWORTH, J. B. *Housing in Transition*, Heinemann, 1963.

DEPARTMENT OF ECONOMIC AFFAIRS. *The West Midlands – A Regional Study*, H.M.S.O., 1965.

DEPARTMENT OF ECONOMIC AFFAIRS *The North-West – A Regional Study*, H.M.S.O., 1965.

DEVEREUX, E. C. 'Neighbourhood and Community Participation', *J. Soc. Issues*, vol. 16, no. 4 (1960), pp. 64–84.

DOUGLAS, J. W. B. and BLOMFIELD, J. M. *Children under Five*, Allen & Unwin, 1958

EDWARDS, A. L. *Statistical Methods for the Behavioural Sciences*, Holt, Rinehart, 1966.

FELLIN, P. and LITWAK, E. 'Neighbourhood Cohesion under Conditions of Mobility', *Am. Sociol. Rev.*, vol. 28, no. 3 (1963), pp. 364–76.

FESTINGER, L., SCHACHTER, S. and BACK, K. *Social Pressures in Informal Groups*, Tavistock, 1963 (first publ. 1950).

FIRTH, R. 'Family and Kinship in Industrial Society', *Sociol. Rev. Monograph*, no. 8 (1964), pp. 65–87.

FLETCHER, R. *The Family and Marriage in Britain*, Penguin, 1966.

FRIEDLANDER, D. and ROSHIER, R. J. 'Internal Migration in England and Wales. Part II: Recent Internal Migrants – their Movements and Characteristics', *Population Studies*, vol. 20, no. 1 (1966), pp. 45–60.

GANS, H. J. 'Planning and Social Life', *J. Am. Inst. Planners*, vol. 27, no. 2 (1961), pp. 134–40.

GANS, H. J. 'The Balanced Community: Homogeneity or Heterogeneity in Residential Areas?' *ibid.*, vol. 27, no. 3 (1961), pp. 176–84.

GANS, H. J. *The Levittowners*, Allen Lane, The Penguin Press, 1967.

GAVRON, H. *The Captive Wife*, Routledge, 1966

GLASS, R. 'Urban Sociology in Great Britain: A Trend Report', *Current Sociol.*, vol. 4, no. 4 (1955), p. 5 *et seq.*

GOLDTHORPE, J. H. and LOCKWOOD, D. 'Not So Bourgeois After All', *New Society*, vol. 1, no. 3 (18 Oct. 1962), pp. 18–19.

GOLDTHORPE, J. H. and LOCKWOOD, D. 'Affluence and the British Class Structure', *Sociol. Rev.* (new series), vol. 11, no. 2 (1963), pp. 133–63.

GOLDTHORPE, J. H., LOCKWOOD, D., BECHHOFER, F. and PLATT, J. 'The Affluent Worker and the Thesis of Embourgeoisement: Some Preliminary Research Findings', *Sociology*, vol. 1, no. 1 (1967) pp. 11–31.

GUTMAN, R. 'Site Planning and Social Behaviour', *J. Soc. Issues*, vol. 22, no. 4 (1966), pp. 103–15.

HALL, J. and JONES, D. CARADOG 'Social Grading of Occupations', *Brit. J. Sociol.*, vol. 1 (1950), pp. 31–55.

HODGES, M. W. and SMITH, C. S. 'The Sheffield Estate' in *Neighbourhood and Community*, Social Research Series, Liverpool University Press, 1954.

HOMANS, G. C. *The Human Group*, Routledge, 1965 (first pub. 1951).

JOHNSTON, J. *Econometric Methods*, McGraw-Hill, 1963.

JONES, M. *Potbank*, Secker & Warburg, 1961.

KATZ, L. and POWELL, J. H. 'A Proposed Index of Conformity of One Sociometric Measurement to Another', in Moreno, J. L. *The Sociometry Reader*, Free Press of Glencoe, 1960, pp. 298–306.

KLEIN, J. *Samples from English Cultures*, vol. 1, Routledge, 1965.

KLEIN, V. *Britain's Married Women Workers*, Routledge, 1965.

KUPER, B. *Privacy and Private Housing*, study financed by R.I.B.A. and Building Design Partnership, 1968.

KUPER, L. 'Blueprint for Living Together', in Kuper, L. (ed.) *Living in Towns*, Cresset, 1953.

LINTON, R. 'The Natural History of the Family' in Anshen, R. *The Family: its Functions and Destiny*, Harper Bros., 1949.

LITWAK, E. 'Occupational Mobility and Extended Family Cohesion', *Am. Sociol. Rev.*, vol. 25, no. 1 (1960), pp. 9–21.

LITWAK, E. 'Geographical Mobility and Extended Family Cohesion', *ibid.*, vol. 25, no. 3 (1960), pp. 385–94.

MACKENZIE, G. 'The Economic Dimensions of Embourgeoisement', *Brit. J. Sociol.*, vol. 18, no. 1. (1967), pp. 29–44.

MERTON, R. K. 'The Social Psychology of Housing', in Dennis, W. *et. al. Current Trends in Social Psychology*, Pittsburgh University Press, 1951, pp. 163–217.

MINISTRY OF HOUSING AND LOCAL GOVERNMENT *Homes for Today and Tomorrow*, H.M.S.O., 1966 (first publ. 1961).

MINISTRY OF HOUSING AND LOCAL GOVERNMENT 'Permanent Houses Completed: England and Wales', in *Annual Abstract of Statistics*, no. 103, H.M.S.O., 1966.

MINISTRY OF HOUSING AND LOCAL GOVERNMENT 'Building Societies: Number of Mortgages by Age of Borrower', *Housing Statistics: Great Britain*, no. 9, H.M.S.O., Apr. 1968, Table 44, p. 52.

MOGEY, J. M. *Family and Neighbourhood*, Oxford University Press, 1956.

MORENO, J. L. (ed.) *The Sociometry Reader*, Free Press of Glencoe, 1960.

MORRIS, R. N. and MOGEY, J. *The Sociology of Housing*, Routledge, 1965.

MUSGROVE, F. *The Migratory Elite*, Heinemann, 1963.

OPPENHEIM, A. N. *Questionnaire Design and Attitude Measurement*, Heinemann, 1966.

PARSONS, T. 'The Social Structure of the Family', in Anshen, R. *The Family: its Functions and Destiny*, Harper Bros, 1949.

PARSONS, T. 'A Revised Analytical Approach to the Theory of Social Stratification', in Bendix R. and Lipset, S. M. *Class, Status and Power*, Free Press of Glencoe, 1953.

QUENOUILLE, M. H. *Introductory Statistics*, Butterworth-Springer, 1950.

ROSOW, I. 'The Social Effects of the Physical Environment', *J. Am. Inst. Planners*, vol. 27, no. 2 (1961), pp. 127–33.

ROSSER, C. and HARRIS, C. C. *The Family and Social Change*, Routledge, 1965.

ROSSI, P. H. *Why Families Move: A Study in the Social Psychology of Urban Residential Mobility*, Free Press of Glencoe, 1955.

SHANKLAND COX and Associates, *Private Housing in London*, Wates, 1969.

SIEGEL, S. *Nonparametric Statistics for the Behavioural Sciences*, McGraw-Hill, 1956.

SMILLIE, K. W. *An Introduction to Regression and Correlation*, Academic Press, 1966.

SNEDECOR, G. W. and COCHRAN, W. G. *Statistical Methods*, Iowa State University Press, 1967 (first publ. 1937).

STAFFORDSHIRE COUNTY COUNCIL *The Development Plan – Town Maps 22 and 23: Survey Report and Analysis*, 1965.

SUSSER, M. and WATSON, A. *Sociology in Medicine*, Oxford University Press, 1962.

SUTCLIFFE, J. P. and CRABBE, B. D. 'Friendship in Urban and Rural Areas', *Social Forces*, vol. 42, no. 1 (1963), pp. 61–7.

WALLIN, P. 'A Guttman Scale for Measuring Women's Neighbourliness', *Am. Jour. Sociol.*, vol. 59 (1953), pp. 243–6.

WHYTE, W. H. *The Organization Man*, Penguin, 1960 (first publ. 1956).

WILKINSON, R. 'Building Society Statistics: A Review Article' *Urban Studies*, vol 2, no. 2 (1965), pp. 186–92.

WILLMOTT, P. and YOUNG, M. *Family and Class in a London Suburb*, Routledge, 1960.

WILLMOTT, P. *The Evolution of a Community*, Routledge, 1963.

YOUNG, M. and WILLMOTT, P. *Family and Kinship in East London*, Penguin, 1965 (first publ. 1957).

GLOSSARY OF STATISTICAL TERMS

G1 *Variable*

If we consider an homogeneous group of objects, say some apples, we may wish to record the weight of each apple. In this sense weight would be a variable, i.e. we would obtain a list of weights varying over the group of apples. Since apples are obviously different, other variables we might derive are circumference, percentage of area which is red, acidity, sugar content, etc., etc. Although some apples would measure up the same as others there would be a spread of values on each attribute and so each attribute measure is a variable.

Variables can be divided into *dependent* and *independent* variables. Suppose that a given variety of apple becomes increasingly sweet with length of storage time. Obviously sweetness depends on storage length and we say that here sweetness is a dependent variable and storage length an independent one. Whether a given variable is one or the other depends essentially on the context of the experiment. Of course, in other situations apple sweetness could be an independent variable.

G2 *Normal Distribution*

If we take any variable, say the weight of Bramley apples, then all Bramley apples grown in Britain during a given year constitute a *population*. If, by some superhuman activity we measure all the weights of all of these fruits in grams we could group apples by weight. We would find that the frequency of the smaller weights and the larger weights would be low, but the middle range weights would be numerous. If we went on to draw a graph of apple weight against the frequency with which each weight occurred the result would be something like the diagram overleaf. This bell-shaped curve is the Normal Curve and if we select large groups from normally-distributed populations by random means we obtain a *random sample*. The shape of the distribution is much the same for the large sample as it is for the parent population. This normal distribution is a remarkable thing as it is very frequently found in nature and in social phenomena.

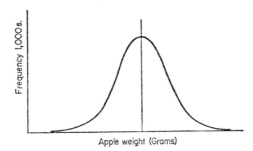

Since it is so common its properties have been exploited in a whole set of statistical tests based upon them. A most useful property of the normal curve is that it may be defined completely by two measures, the first a measure of central tendency, the second a measure of spread. The first measure is the *mean*, the second is the *standard deviation*.

G3 *The Arithmetic Mean*

This is the simple average we use in everyday life. In statistics it is written as μ (for a population mean), $\bar{X}$ (for a sample mean)

$$\text{symbolically } \mu = \frac{\Sigma X_i}{n}$$

This is to say that the population mean is the sum of (Σ) all the values of the variable X_i (say, the weights of all the apples) divided by the number of the apples weighed.

The Standard Deviation

This is formalised as σ (population) or as s (sample)

$$\sigma = \sqrt{\frac{\Sigma(\mu - X_i)^2}{n}}$$

that is to say each value of the variable is subtracted from the population mean. All deviations are squared and the sum of the squared deviations are obtained. This sum is then divided by the number of values and the square root is taken. The old name for σ is 'root mean squared deviation' and this summarises the operation in words.

G4   *Sum of squares*

This is a derived measure which appears a lot in statistics, it is in fact nothing more complicated than the numerator of the standard deviation expression i.e. $(\mu - X_i)^2$; or for a sample, $(\overline{X} - X_i)^2$

G5   *Variance*

The variance is the square of the standard deviation, thus

$$\sigma^2 = \frac{\Sigma(\mu - X_i)^2}{n}$$

Apart from being a measure which forms the basis of a number of tests, variance is of considerable conceptual importance. Since the spread of variables around a central value defines the behaviour of a sample, the derivation of hypotheses and associated tests which seek to explain this variance is of paramount importance in the understanding of social and other processes.

G6   *Degrees of Freedom*

This is a difficult concept. At the most elementary level the concept is best illustrated by the formula for the standard deviation in a *sample*. Here the denominator in the expression is $n-1$ rather than n. The reason for this is illustrated by an example. Suppose we have a very small sample of five observations and we know (in some magical way) that the mean is 7. Then four only of the observations are free to vary the fifth one must make the necessary adjustments to bring the mean back again to 7. Consequently, there are only four degrees of freedom. This may seem a trifling point but it *is* rather important when the sample size is small.

G7 *Statistical Significance*

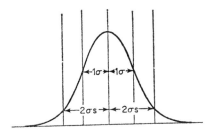

As indicated earlier the normal curve has a universal applicability defined in terms of the mean and standard deviation only. The normal distribution has other useful properties: if a distribution is truly normal 68·3 per cent of all observations lie within one standard deviation from the mean, 95·5 per cent of all observations lie within two standard deviations each way from the mean. An important measure is 1·96σ because these ordinates enclose 95 per cent of observations.

The above facts are related to probability and statistical significance. One important point in statistics is that we can rarely be 100 per cent sure of something, as we can in a subject like chemistry. Consequently we accept a known risk of being wrong. As an example suppose we have a single apple and we do not know whether or not it is a Bramley, for which we have a distribution of weights. We might then be prepared to accept weight as the criterion for the single apple being a Bramley and we weigh it. Now as the Normal Curve is asymptotic, there is a probability of 1·0 of the apple's weight being under the curve. However, the apple might still belong to another population of a (say) heavier variety with a mean somewhere along the weight axis to the right. Accordingly, in order to make probalistic statements in statistics we pre-select probability levels. For example, if we exclude apple weights more than 1·96σ from the mean we run a 5 per cent risk of being wrong by chance alone. In this instance, then, we would exclude the apple from membership of the Bramley variety if its weight be less or greater than 1·96σ from the mean of Bramleys, and we could be 95 per cent sure of being right in so doing.

G8   *Skew Distributions*

Sometimes the frequency distribution of variables is not sym-metrical about the mean – it is lop-sided. In such cases the usual properties and associated tests break down and it is necessary to take the steps adopted in the next section.

G9   *Transformation*

If one has a skew distribution or if one wishes to relate two variables using a linear model and yet the real relationship is curvilinear then it is necessary to treat the data first. Such treatments, aimed at making distributions more symmetrical or relationships more linear, are known as transformations. For example one could very well achieve these ends by operating on the logarithms of each value or one might transform each to its reciprocal. The usual tests are then carried out on the trans-formed data. There is nothing irregular in such procedures since the transformed data bears a known and constant relationship to the raw data.

G10   *t-test*

This is a statistical test which deals with the significance of the difference between the means of two samples. If two random sample means are so different that we suspect that this difference is significant in the statistical sense, this infers that the two samples are from two different populations. If the populations are different the variances are also likely to be different, accordingly the *t*-test is a test of the magnitude of the differences between means taking the variances into account. It ends up with state-ments such as 'we are 95 per cent sure that the mean of sample 1 is greater than sample 2.'

G11   *Analysis of Variance and F test*

The analysis of variance is a generalisation of the *t*-test in that it provides a method for the examination of the significance between the means of *n* samples simultaneously. While it would be possible to investigate this by repetitive *t*-testing this is hazardous since we are likely to find significant differences *by chance alone*. Analysis of variance gives other facilities as well, for instance our samples might be capable of subdivision in terms of the sex of the individuals comprising them. If this was so, we could investigate two effects at the same time: the significance of differences between samples ignoring sex and the significance due to sex ignoring samples. More complex undertakings are possible and are used, especially in the field of educational research. The relevant statistic which is tested is the variance ratio or F test, this is analogous to the *t*-test but it is applicable to the *n* sample situation.

G12   *Chi-squared test* (χ^2)

This is the most elementary statistical test used by sociologists. It is a test of inter-varietal differences. It is also a test of association. For example we might hypothesise that old people attend church more frequently than young ones. Accordingly, we could define our terms, mount a survey and interpret our results. A result might be

	Church Attendance	
	Rare	*Frequent*
Old	20	40
Young	40	10

That is, we interviewed 110 people and asked them their ages and details of church attendance with the above results expressed in a contingency table. It is pretty obvious that old people are more assiduous attenders and we would be pretty safe in stating this as a fact. However, the balance is not always as pronounced in sociology and we are often in doubt as to whether a second randomly selected group would display a similar distribution; or expressed otherwise, whether the imbalance is purely a function of chance. χ^2 helps us to attach a known level of risk to our research interpretations.

G13   *Correlation Coefficient (r)*

This statistic is a most useful one and is a sophisticated extension of χ^2. It is easily grasped. Supposing we were relating peoples' heights and weights. Obviously we expect taller people to be heavier and vice versa. Of course there will usually be exceptions, then we say that the correlation between height and weight or whatever is less than perfect. If a correlation between two variables is perfect then the coefficient for a random bivariate sample is denoted by ρ and is $+1$ or -1. If there is no correlation then the value is 0. The correlation coefficient, then, measures the degree of perfection in covariation between two variables. If the variables are measured at a lower order metric (say, ranked) then a coefficient of rank correlation is used. The most popular of these is Spearman's, usually written as ρ_s.

G14   *Partial Correlation*

The existence of a high degree of correlation between the values of two variables does not imply that one is necessarily dependent on the other. The literature is full of nonsense correlations which are nothing more than artifacts. However, social scientists usually have a well established theoretical background before they undertake an empirical study and the correlations they obtain are usually strategically important. Nevertheless, it doesn't matter how well based they are in theory, high correlations still do not imply causality. The reason for this is that the majority of correlations turn out to be spurious. The high correlation between X and Y may be entirely due to the effect of Z. If we wish to isolate the real degree of association between X and Y, we must hold Z constant. This process is known as 'partialling out the effect of Z'. The correlation coefficient between X and Y, partialling out the effect of Z is written $\gamma_{xy \cdot z}$. In sociology variables overlap to such an extent that $\gamma_{xy \cdot z}$ is usually considerably smaller than the original γ_{xy}.

G15   *Multiple Regression*

This is a technique where the variability of a single variable is seen as a linear combination of a number of independent variables

$$\Upsilon = f(X_1 + X_2 + - - - - - - X_n)$$

This is to say that the dependent variable (Υ) is a function (f) of X_1 through to X_n. More rigorously

$$\Upsilon = a + \beta_1 X_1 + \beta_2 X_2 + - - - - - - - - + \beta_n X_n$$

Here the betas are the population regression coefficients of weights and they are partial coefficients. Hence the coefficient for X_1 is $\beta_{yx_1.x_2 - - - - .x}$. From the derivation, by the computer of these coefficients we can determine what percentage of the variance of Υ is explained by each of the independent variables. We might find that β_2 is not significant, statistically; and this would mean that X_2 may be dropped as it adds nothing to our understanding of the behaviour of Υ.

G16 *Dummy Variable*

In the preceding statistical model, the variables are assumed to be measured at a fairly sophisticated level, e.g. inches, grams, etc. The problem in sociology is to measure at the most sophisticated level possible. Not only does this give better confidence in the making of decisions but it does not abuse the statistical methods used. Obviously if we have peoples' heights recorded in inches we are not going to divide the sample into tall and short depending on a dichotomy about the mean height. This would be a disservice to the data and would sacrifice discriminatory power. However, we are often faced with measurement which is very primitive. An example of such a primitive scale of measurement is the nominal scale. On this scale all we might have is the information, say, that people are British or non-British and one cannot be 1.25 British, or whatever. Traditionally, data measured nominally has been analysed by χ^2; but this is a weakish tool. Often we want to bring such a scale within a more rewarding statistical model e.g. multiple regression. If we do, and we have an extra measure such as British or not, it has been shown that a dummy variable may be used to take account of it. In such cases we may score 1 for British or 0 for non-British and embody these scores in the regression model.

Index